Quattro
Their

Function Keys	Macro Equivalent
F1	Help; no macro keyword
F2	{edit}
Shift-F2	{step}
F3	{name}
G F3	Properties sheet; no macro keyword
* Alt-F3	{functions}
* Shift-F3	{macros}
F4	{abs}
F5	{goto}
* Alt-F5	{undo}
* Shift-F5 or Alt-0	{choose}
F6	{window}
* Alt-F6	{zoom}
* Shift-F6	{nextwin}
F7	{query}
G F7	Proportional resize; no macro keyword
F Alt-F7	{markall}
G Shift-F7	Select; no macro keyword
F * Shift-F7	{mark}
F8	{table}
F * Shift-F8	{move}
F9	{calc}
F * F9	{readdir}
F * Shift-F9	{copy}
F10	{graph}
F * Shift-F10	{paste}
Ctrl-F10	{pdxgo}

The Sybex Instant Reference Series

Instant References are available on these topics:

AutoCAD Release 11

dBASE

dBASE III PLUS Programming

dBASE IV Programming

dBASE IV 1.1

DESQview

DOS

DOS 5

Harvard Graphics

Harvard Graphics 3

Lotus 1-2-3 Release 2.2

Lotus 1-2-3 Release 2.3

Macintosh Software

Microsoft Word for the Macintosh

Microsoft Word for the PC

Norton Desktop for Windows

Norton Utilities 5

Norton Utilities 6

PageMaker 4.0 for the Macintosh

Paradox 3.5

PC Tools Deluxe 6

Windows 3.0

WordPerfect 5

WordPerfect 5.1

Computer users are not all alike.
Neither are SYBEX books.

We know our customers have a variety of needs. They've told us so. And because we've listened, we've developed several distinct types of books to meet the needs of each of our customers. What are you looking for in computer help?

If you're looking for the basics, try the **ABC's** series, or for a more visual approach, select **Teach Yourself.**

Mastering and **Understanding** titles offer you a step-by-step introduction, plus an in-depth examination of intermediate-level features, to use as you progress.

Our **Up & Running** series is designed for computer-literate consumers who want a no-nonsense overview of new programs. Just 20 basic lessons, and you're on your way.

SYBEX **Encyclopedias** and **Desktop References** provide a *comprehensive reference* and explanation of all of the commands, features, and functions of the subject software.

Sometimes a subject requires a special treatment that our standard series doesn't provide. So you'll find we have titles like **Advanced Techniques, Handbooks, Tips & Tricks,** and others that are specifically tailored to satisfy a unique need.

You'll find SYBEX publishes a variety of books on every popular software package. Looking for computer help? Help Yourself to SYBEX.

For a complete catalog of our publications:

SYBEX, Inc.
2021 Challenger Drive, Alameda, CA 94501
Tel: (510) 523-8233/(800) 227-2346 Telex: 336311
Fax: (510) 523-2373

SYBEX is committed to using natural resources wisely to preserve and improve our environment. This is why we have been printing the text of books like this one on recycled paper since 1982.

This year our use of recycled paper will result in the saving of more than 15,300 trees. We will lower air pollution effluents by 54,000 pounds, save 6,300,000 gallons of water, and reduce landfill by 2,700 cubic yards.

In choosing a SYBEX book you are not only making a choice for the best in skills and information, you are also choosing to enhance the quality of life for all of us.

Quattro® Pro 3 Instant Reference

Gene Weisskopf

SYBEX®

San Francisco • Paris • Düsseldorf • Soest

Acquisitions Editor: Dianne King
Series Editor: James A. Compton
Copy Editors: Jeff Kapellas and Savitha Varadan
Technical Editor: Glenn Y. Saika
Word Processors: Ann Dunn and Susan Trybull
Paste Up Artist: Claudia Smelser
Screen Graphics: Cuong Le
Typesetter: Deborah Maizels
Proofreaders: Lisa Haden and Catherine Mahoney
Indexer: Tom McFadden
Cover Designer: Archer Design
Screen reproductions produced by XenoFont.

XenoFont is a trademark of XenoSoft.

SYBEX is a registered trademark of SYBEX, Inc.

TRADEMARKS: SYBEX has attempted throughout this book to distinguish proprietary trademarks from descriptive terms by following the capitalization style used by the manufacturer.

SYBEX is not affiliated with any manufacturer.

Every effort has been made to supply complete and accurate information. However, SYBEX assumes no responsibility for its use, nor for any infringement of the intellectual property rights of third parties which would result from such use.

Copyright ©1991 SYBEX Inc., 2021 Challenger Drive, Alameda, CA 94501. World rights reserved. No part of this publication may be stored in a retrieval system, transmitted, or reproduced in any way, including but not limited to photocopy, photograph, magnetic or other record, without the prior agreement and written permission of the publisher.

Library of Congress Card Number: 91-66107
ISBN: 0-89588-822-X

Manufactured in the United States of America
10 9 8 7 6 5 4 3 2 1

To my older brother, Alan, whose influence can't be measured or overemphasized (try as he might)

Acknowledgments

As usual, I extend my appreciation to those at SYBEX who worked to ensure that this book is attractive, grammatically and technically accurate, and produced in a timely manner. My thanks go as well to Dianne King, Acquisitions Editor, for her willingness to listen and respond to my queries.

At Borland, thanks are in order to Nan Borreson for helping me stay in touch with the spreadsheet activity there; to Tami Casey and Anne Quackenbush for their work in connecting Borland and user groups; and to Robert Stout, in Borland Technical Support, for his willingness to research my questions.

The members of the Sacramento PC Users Group get my continuing appreciation, with special acknowledgment going to Larry and Mary Clark, chief and managing editors of the Group's newsletter, *Sacra Blue*. When they accepted the task of editing the newsletter, they took on a mandate to uphold a longstanding tradition of excellence. They have succeeded in keeping that tradition alive and well.

My warm appreciation also goes to those in the Davis Chapter of the Group, especially Tim Feldman, the chapter's new president.

Finally, a certain recognition goes to those in Sacramento, California, whom as a result of my new bicoastal existence I will see less frequently, and to those in Pendleton, South Carolina, whom I have yet to meet.

Table of Contents

Introduction

xix

Part I
OVERVIEW OF QUATTRO PRO

Installing Quattro Pro	**2**
Starting Quattro Pro	**4**
The Quattro Pro Screen	**4**
Moving the Cursor from the Keyboard	**6**
Keystrokes for Editing	**7**
Using a Mouse	**7**
Accessing the Menus	**9**
Getting Help	**10**

Part II
SPREADSHEET OPERATIONS

Database–Data Entry	**16**
Database–Paradox Access	**17**
Database–Query	**18**
Assign Names	**18**
Block	**19**
Criteria Table	**20**
Delete	**22**
Extract	**22**
Locate	**23**
Output Block	**24**

Reset	25
Unique	25
Database–Restrict Input	26
Database–Sort	27
Sort Rules	29
Edit–Copy	30
Edit–Delete	31
Edit–Erase Block	32
Edit–Fill	33
Edit–Insert	34
Edit–Move	35
Edit–Names	36
Create	36
Delete	37
Labels	37
Reset	38
Make Tables	39
Edit–Search & Replace	39
Edit–Transpose	42
Edit–Undo	43
Edit–Values	43
File–Close	44
File–Close All	45
File–Directory	46
File–Erase	47
File–Exit	48
File–New	49
File–Open	49
File–Retrieve	52
File–Save	53
File–Save All (Version 3 Only)	55
File–Save As	57

File–Utilities	58
DOS Shell	58
File Manager	60
SQZ!	60
File–Workspace	62
Graph–Annotate	63
Graph–Customize Series	63
Bar Width	63
Colors	64
Fill Patterns	64
Interior Labels	64
Markers & Lines	64
Override Type	65
Pies	65
Reset	66
Update	66
Y-axis	66
Graph–Fast Graph	67
Graph–Graph Type	69
Graph–Hide	71
Graph–Insert	71
Graph–Name	73
Autosave Edits (Version 3 Only)	73
Create	73
Display	74
Erase	75
Graph Copy	75
Reset	76
Slide	76
Graph–Overall	77
Graph–Series	79
Graph–Text	80

Graph–View	83
Graph–X-Axis and Graph–Y-Axis	84
Options–Colors	86
Options–Display Mode	87
Options–Formats	88
Options–Graphics Quality	89
Options–Hardware	91
Memory Status	91
Mouse Button (Version 3 Only)	91
Printers	92
Screen	94
Options–International	95
Options–Mouse Palette	97
Options–Other	98
Options–Protection	100
Options–Recalculation	100
Options–Startup	102
Options–Update	103
Options–Values (Version 3 Only)	104
Options–WYSIWYG Zoom % (Version 3 Only)	104
Print–Adjust Printer	105
Print–Block	105
Print–Copies (Version 3 Only)	106
Print–Destination	107
Print–Format	110
Print–Graph Print	111
Print–Headings	113
Print–Layout	114
Print–Print To Fit (Version 3 Only)	118
Print–Spreadsheet Print	119
Style–Alignment	120

Style–Block Size	121
Style–Column Width	124
Style–Font	125
Style–Hide Column	126
Style–Insert Break	127
Style–Line Drawing	128
Style–Numeric Format	129
Style–Protection	132
Style–Reset Width	133
Style–Shading	134
Tools–Advanced Math	135
Invert	135
Multiply	135
Optimization	136
Regression	137
Tools–Combine	139
Tools–Frequency	140
Tools–Import	141
Tools–Macro	143
Clear Breakpoints	143
Debugger	143
Execute	145
Instant Replay	145
Key Reader	145
Library	145
Macro Recording	146
Name	146
Paste	146
Record	147
Transcript	147
Tools–Parse	148
Tools–Reformat	150

Tools–Solve For	150
Tools–Update Links	151
Tools–What-if	152
Tools–Xtract	155
Window–Move/Size	156
Window–Options	158
Window–Pick	161
Window–Stack	161
Window–Tile	162
Window–Zoom	162

Part III

THE GRAPH ANNOTATOR

Arrow	166
Clipboard	167
Ellipse	168
Help	170
Line	170
Link	170
Pick	171
Polygon	175
Polyline	175
Quit	177
Rectangle	177
Text	178
Vertical/Horizontal Line	180

Part IV

THE FILE MANAGER

Edit–Copy	**186**
Edit–Duplicate	**187**
Edit–Erase	**187**
Edit–Move	**188**
Edit–Paste	**188**
Edit–Rename	**189**
Edit–Select File and Edit–All Select	**189**
File–Open	**190**
File–Make Dir	**190**
File–Read Dir	**191**
Options–File List	**191**
Options–Startup–Directory	**192**
Print–Block	**192**
Sort	**193**
Tree	**193**

Part V

@ FUNCTIONS

Mathematical Functions	**199**
Statistical Functions	**202**
Table Lookup Functions	**204**
Spreadsheet Information Functions	**207**
String Functions	**208**
Date and Time Functions	**212**
Financial Functions	**216**

Logical Functions	221
Database Functions	223
System Functions	225

Part VI
MACRO COMMANDS

Screen Control	230
User Interaction	231
Program Control	235
Cell Manipulation	237
Text Files	239

Index

242

Introduction

Borland International first released Quattro Pro in the latter months of 1989, into a market dominated by one spreadsheet, Lotus 1-2-3. While industry observers speculated on the odds for success of yet another spreadsheet, Quattro Pro quickly established itself as the spreadsheet that the competition had to match.

Within two years of the first release of the program, Borland shipped releases 2, SE, and 3, enhancing and fine-tuning this acclaimed program. Spreadsheet users have found many key items from their wish-list implemented in Quattro Pro 3:

- The ability to work with multiple spreadsheets, and link data among them
- A true WYSIWYG display (for EGA and VGA systems) that shows all fonts and spreadsheet enhancements
- Presentation-quality spreadsheet output
- Tools for creating and presenting slide shows with slide transition effects as well as sound effects
- Enhanced graphs and highly advanced graphing tools
- Reasonable memory requirements
- Complete Lotus 1-2-3 version 2.2 file and command compatibility, including a "soft" interface with Lotus 1-2-3 and Quattro menus
- The Paradox Access, which allows you to run both Paradox and Quattro Pro at the same time, integrating the power of each without sacrificing performance

Who Should Read This Book *Quattro Pro 3 Instant Reference* provides a ready reference for Quattro Pro users of all levels of expertise. If you consider yourself a spreadsheet novice, you can quickly look up a new and unfamiliar command in this alphabetized reference. Each reference contains plenty of information to get you started down the learning path. For the more accomplished spreadsheet user, a glance through these pages will serve to refresh your memory or extend your knowledge of Quattro Pro features.

Most of the information in the command references apply to versions 2, SE, and 3 of Quattro Pro, and you will find this instant reference useful regardless of which version you own. Information that applies to only one version will be clearly marked.

If you are already a user of Quattro or Lotus 1-2-3, you should find the transition to Quattro Pro to be both effortless and exciting. You will be able to load up to 32 of your existing spreadsheet files into Quattro Pro at one time and begin to take advantage of its extensive features right away.

How This Book Is Organized The various commands and features of Quattro Pro have been divided among the six parts of this book:

- Part I serves as an introduction to Quattro Pro 3. It offers tips on software installation, starting the program, the parts of the spreadsheet, the menu system, navigating the spreadsheet with the keyboard or a mouse, and manipulating blocks in the spreadsheet. If you are a newcomer to Quattro Pro, you'll want to read this part right away.

- Part II covers all the commands on the spreadsheet menus and is, therefore, the largest part in this book.

- Part III will help you enhance your graphs with the Graph Annotator.

- Part IV shows you the commands and features of the File Manager, which helps you access and organize your spreadsheet and other files.

- Part V lists all of the @ functions in Quattro Pro, arranged by category in order of appearance on the Quattro Pro functions list (Alt-F3).

- Part VI does the same for Quattro Pro's macro command language in their order of appearance on the Quattro Pro macro list (Shift-F3).

Menu commands in each part are listed alphabetically so that, for example, when you want to learn about the Copy command on the Edit menu, simply turn to Part II and look up Edit and then Copy.

To invoke a command in Quattro Pro, you must frequently choose commands from several menus. In this book, a series of commands may be shown as one long chain, with a dash between each step, such as Style–Font–Edit Fonts. The actual selections you make from the menus or information you type in from the keyboard are shown in boldface, such as **Copy**. If there is a shortcut for a command, it will be shown in parentheses after the command, such as **Copy** (Ctrl-C). Long command lines and program examples will appear on a separate line in a different typeface, such as

@IPAYMT (0.11/12,1,30*12,125000)

The screens shown in most of the figures in this book were captured while Quattro Pro was in text mode. If you are used to the high speed of the standard text-mode display of a DOS computer, you may find that working in graphics mode just feels too slow. Therefore, you may want to run Quattro Pro in text mode, and realize that you can switch to graphics mode (if you have an EGA or VGA display) at any time with the Options–Display Mode–WYSIWYG command.

Part I

An Overview of Quattro Pro

This part of *Quattro Pro 3 Instant Reference* will introduce you to the program as a whole and includes some notes on installation, starting the program, the parts of a spreadsheet, navigating a spreadsheet with the keyboard or a mouse, and accessing the menus and help systems.

2 An Overview of Quattro Pro

INSTALLING QUATTRO PRO

You will need all your Quattro Pro program disks for the installation routine, as well as five megabytes of free space on your hard disk. Put the first Quattro Pro disk in your floppy disk drive and make that drive the default by typing **A:** (if you are using your A drive) and pressing ↵. Then type **INSTALL** and press ↵ to start the installation routine.

Respond to the routine's prompts, and insert each of the program disks into the drive when you are directed to. When all program files have been copied to your hard disk, you will be prompted to answer several questions about Quattro Pro's configuration for your computer system. If you want to enter information or change the default choice, press F2 and then enter the information.

- *Monitor Type*: If you have a color video card, you will need to specify whether your monitor is Color (the default), Black and White, or Gray Scale.

- *Company Name*: Press F2 and enter your company name, which will appear on Quattro Pro's log-on screen each time you start the program. Just enter something like **Personal** if this is your personal copy of the program.

- *Name*: Enter your name, which will also appear on Quattro Pro's log-in screen.

- *Serial #*: Enter the program's serial number, which you will find on Disk 1 of the Quattro Pro program disks.

- *Are you installing Quattro Pro on a network server?*: Choose No if your computer is not connected to a network. If it is on a network, you should contact your network administrator for assistance before you choose Yes.

- *Edit AUTOEXEC.BAT file?*: Install asks if you want it to edit your AUTOEXEC.BAT file and include your new Quattro Pro subdirectory in the PATH command. Generally, you should choose No for this option. Later, you can simply change to Quattro Pro's subdirectory before you start the program.

- *User Interface*: Accept the default setting to use Quattro Pro's standard menu system. Once you are running

Quattro Pro, you can always use the Options–Startup–Menu Tree command to change to a different menu tree.

- *Printer Manufacturer*: Select your printer's manufacturer from the list that is offered.

- *Printer Model*: Select your printer's model from the list.

- *Printer Mode*: Depending on the printer you have selected, you may be offered a choice of print resolutions for graphics printouts, such as 100×100 or 200×200. Choose the highest density for now. You can later use the Options–Hardware–Printer's command to change the settings for the selected printer.

- *WYSIWYG Mode*: You can choose Yes to load Quattro Pro in WYSIWYG (graphics) mode, but it is recommended that you choose No and have Quattro Pro run in text mode, which is much faster than graphics mode. Either way, you can later use the Options–Display Mode command to switch to a different display mode.

- *Install Quattro Pro for Windows?*: If you have Microsoft Windows (version 3 or later) installed on your hard disk, choose Yes to have Install create a program group and icon for Quattro Pro. You will be prompted for the location of Windows on your hard disk, such as C:\WIN.

- *Bitstream Character Set*: Quattro Pro uses Bitstream downloadable fonts when you print to your graphics printer. Choose which character set you want to use, either Standard U.S. or Standard European. There are more characters in the European set, so those fonts will take about 20 percent more disk space.

- *Fonts to Build*: You can create a set of Bitstream soft fonts that will be stored on disk in your Quattro Pro subdirectory. You can skip this step for now by choosing None. When you are printing in Final quality mode, it will build any fonts that are needed and store them on disk.

The Install program will build any fonts you have selected, and then return you to the DOS prompt, from which you can run Quattro Pro.

STARTING QUATTRO PRO

If you installed Quattro Pro on your C drive in the subdirectory named QPRO, do the following to start the program from the DOS prompt:

1. Type **C:** and press ↵ to make that drive the default.
2. Type **CD\QPRO** and press ↵ to make that subdirectory the default.
3. Type **Q** and press ↵ to start the program.

The Quattro Pro spreadsheet will appear on the screen, and you will be ready to get to work.

If your computer has expanded (EMS) memory, and you don't specify otherwise when you start Quattro Pro, the program will allocate all that memory for its own use. This not only lets you create larger spreadsheets, but it also speeds up many of the Quattro Pro program routines.

In Quattro Pro 3, if you wish to limit the amount of expanded memory used, use the /En command-line parameter when you start the program. Replace the n with the number of 16-kilobyte blocks of EMS memory that you want Quattro Pro to take. For example, to instruct Quattro Pro to use just 64 KB of EMS memory, use the command **Q/E4**.

To start Quattro Pro and have it automatically load a spreadsheet file, simply append the file's name and, optionally, its location to the startup command (see also the Options–Startup–Autoload File command). For example, to load the file named MYFILE from the DATA directory on your D drive, enter:

Q D:\DATA\MYFILE

THE QUATTRO PRO SCREEN

The Quattro Pro spreadsheet should look familiar if you have used other spreadsheet programs. Even so, you may not recognize a few of its features. Figure I.1 shows the basic Quattro Pro screen.

The *spreadsheet,* or *worksheet,* is made up of rows and columns, which are identified by numbers down the left side of the screen

The Quattro Pro Screen 5

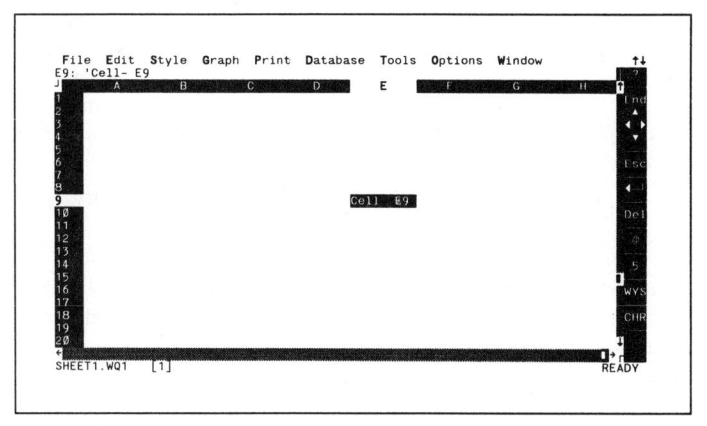

Figure I.1: The Quattro Pro spreadsheet

and letters along the top of the screen. There are 8192 rows in a Quattro Pro spreadsheet, and 256 columns, which are labeled A through IV.

Each cell is identified by its column and row, so that the *address* of the cell at the junction of column E and row 9 is referred to as E9. In Figure I.1, cell E9 has a text entry in it that says *Cell- E9*. You enter data into the cells of the spreadsheet. Each cell is separate and unique from all the other cells, and it can hold a maximum of 254 characters.

The cell selector or cursor is the highlighted bar that shows which cell is the current, or active, cell. The cell selector's current column letter is highlighted at the top of the spreadsheet, and its row number is highlighted to the left of the spreadsheet. This tells you at a glance exactly where the cell selector is in the spreadsheet.

When you type an entry for the current cell, the results of your keystrokes first appear on the *input line*, which is on the second row of the screen. When you press ↵, or move the cell selector to a different cell, the data on the input line is placed into the current cell. When you create or edit an entry that is longer than the input line (76 characters), the line will expand up to four lines so that you can see the entire entry.

Information about the current cell (the one that is highlighted by the cell selector) appears in the input line. In Figure I.1, the cell selector is

6   An Overview of Quattro Pro

on cell E9, and you can see the contents of that cell on the input line, which includes the current cell contents, preceded by the cell address, numeric format, column width, and font.

The bottom line of the screen is the *status line*, where information about the current spreadsheet file is displayed.

In Figure I.1, you can see the file name of the current spreadsheet, SHEET1.WQ1, at the left of the status line.

The window number, [1], next to the name identifies the current window. Each new window that you open in Quattro Pro is assigned a unique number in consecutive order, so that the next window to be opened would be [2], the next [3], and so on.

At the far right on the status line is the mode indicator, where the current mode of the spreadsheet is shown. In Figure I.1, the spreadsheet is in Ready mode. Other modes include Menu, when you are accessing Quattro Pro's menus; Edit, when you are editing a cell; and Value, when you are entering a numeric value into a cell.

MOVING THE CURSOR FROM THE KEYBOARD

You can move the cell selector in several different ways using the keyboard:

- Cursor-control keys: Press either ←, →, ↑, or ↓ to move the cell selector one cell in the indicated direction.
- PgUp: Moves the cell selector up one full screen.
- PgDn: Moves the cell selector down one full screen.
- Tab or Ctrl-→: Moves the cell selector right one full screen.
- Shift-Tab or Ctrl-←: Moves the cell selector left one full screen.
- Function key F5: Press F5, and then type the cell address or block name (see the Edit–Names command) to which you want to go, and then press ↵. The cell selector will jump to that cell.
- Home: Moves the cell selector to cell A1, no matter where it was in the spreadsheet.

- End-Home: Moves the cell selector to the last occupied row and column in the spreadsheet.

- Window–Pick: If you are working with more than one window at a time, you can jump to another window with the Window–Pick command (refer to that command reference).

You can also use the End key to move the cell selector along many cells in a row or column. Press the End key, and the End indicator will appear at the bottom of the screen. Next, press any of the arrow keys, and the cell selector will move as far as it can in the specified direction, based on the following rules:

- If the cell selector is on an occupied cell, it will move in the direction of the arrow to the last occupied cell before a blank cell.

- If the cell selector is on an empty cell, it will move in the direction of the arrow to the first occupied cell.

- If the current cell is occupied and the cell next to it is empty, the cell selector will move to the next occupied cell.

- If all cells in the row or column are blank, the cell selector will move to the last spreadsheet cell of the row or column.

KEYSTROKES FOR EDITING

Table I.1 lists several keystrokes that are available when you are editing text in Quattro Pro. For example, you can use them when you are editing the contents of a cell or changing a file name or path for one of the file-related commands.

USING A MOUSE

You can put a mouse to work in a variety of ways in Quattro Pro, but its use is always optional. You will find the mouse particularly helpful when you are working in the Graph Annotator, when you have multiple windows open and wish to switch from one to another (just click in the window you want), or when you want to move or resize a window (see the Window–Move/Size command).

8 An Overview of Quattro Pro

Whether your mouse has one, two, three, or more buttons, Quattro Pro uses only one button. The left button is the default active button. (For information on changing the mouse button settings, see the Options–Hardware–Mouse Button command reference.) There are three different actions you can perform with the mouse:

- Pointing: Moving the mouse pointer to any part of the screen. For example, point to relocate the cell selector or choose an item from the menus.

- Dragging: Holding down the mouse button and moving the mouse. For example, drag to highlight a block of cells in the spreadsheet.

- Clicking: Giving the mouse button a quick click, generally to select an item to which you are pointing.

Along the right side of the screen is a series of boxes that make up the mouse palette (see Figure I.1). This menu, which appears only if the mouse driver has been installed, is simply an aid for mouse users; it can be accessed only with a mouse. The first item in the palette is a question mark (?). Pointing at the ? and clicking your mouse brings up the Quattro Pro help screens, as though you had pressed F1.

Table I.1: Keystrokes for Editing

Keystroke	Action
Ins	Insert/typeover mode
Del	Delete current character
Backspace	Delete character to left
Home	Beginning of entry
End	End of entry
Ctrl-\	Delete from cursor to end of entry
Escape	Delete entry
Tab or Ctrl-→	Move five characters right
Shift-Tab or Ctrl-←	Move five characters left

The next box, with the word End and the four arrows, moves the cell selector in the direction of the arrow on which you click, as though you had first pressed the End key.

The next four mouse palette boxes perform the same function as the Escape, ↵, Delete, and Alt-F3 (@ functions list) keys, respectively. The box labeled 5 has no action assigned to it. The box beneath it, labeled WYS (for WYSIWYG) switches the display to graphics mode. The last box, labeled CHR (for character), changes the display to text mode (see the Options–Display Mode command).

Together, these seven boxes make up the *programmable* items of the mouse palette. You can change the definition of each of these to suit your own needs (see the Options–Mouse Palette command).

Just to the left of the mouse palette is a vertical shaded bar called the *scroll bar*. When you click on any portion of this bar, the cell selector is moved vertically in the spreadsheet. Another scroll bar is located along the bottom of the spreadsheet. It is used to move the cell selector horizontally. There is a small *scroll box* within each scroll bar. You can move the cell selector by pointing at the scroll box and then dragging it. At either end of each scroll bar is a *scroll arrow*. Clicking on a scroll arrow moves the cell selector one cell at a time in the arrow's direction.

ACCESSING THE MENUS

The menus in Quattro Pro contain the commands for performing practically all the operations that are available in the program, and each of them is discussed in this book.

The menus are in the menu bar across the top of the screen. These are called *pull-down menus* because they "pull down" from the menu bar. Selecting a menu item may either execute the desired command or simply call another menu with more choices. Some Quattro Pro menus are many layers deep.

There are two different ways to access the menus:

- From the Ready mode with keyboard, just press the slash key (/). The first item on the menu bar, File, will be highlighted, meaning the menu bar is now active and waiting for you to make a choice from it.

An Overview of Quattro Pro

- With a mouse, just point to the desired item on the menu bar and click the mouse button. That item's menu will appear, ready for you to make a selection.

After you have activated the menu bar, you can use one of these methods to select an item:

- Using the arrow keys, move the highlight left or right to the command you want to choose, and then press ↵.
- Simply type the highlighted letter of the command (usually the first letter), such as F for File or P for Print.
- With a mouse, point to the item and click the mouse button.

Whenever you are selecting commands from the menu, you can use the Escape key to back out of what you are doing, one step at a time. Or, you can press Ctrl-Break to return to Ready mode in one step.

Many commands on the Quattro Pro menus have *shortcut* keys assigned to them. By using the shortcut, you can choose a command with a single keystroke, no matter how far down the menu tree that command may be. There are two types of shortcut keys in Quattro Pro: function keys (used alone or in conjunction with the Ctrl, Alt, or Shift key) and Ctrl-key combinations. A command's shortcut is listed to the right of the command on the menu. You can assign your own Ctrl-key shortcut to a command by highlighting the command on the menu and pressing Ctrl-↵, and then typing the Ctrl-letter combination you wish for that command.

GETTING HELP

No matter where you are in Quattro Pro, help is available by simply pressing F1 or by clicking on the ? with your mouse. Help is *context sensitive*, so whether you are editing the contents of a cell or moving through the menus, pressing the F1 key will bring up a help screen that gives you relevant information about your position in the program.

All help screens contain certain keywords that are displayed in a different color or highlighted on a monochrome display. You can highlight any one of these, press ↵, and see another screen of information related to the keyword (or just click on a keyword with your mouse).

Getting Help 11

There are just a few keys you will need within the help system:

- ←, →, ↑, or ↓: Moves between the keywords.
- Home: Moves to the first keyword on screen.
- End: Moves to the last keyword on screen.
- F1: Brings up a help screen for the help system.
- Backspace: Shows the previous screen.
- Escape: Returns to the spreadsheet.
- F3: Press F3 twice, and a list of those who helped create Quattro Pro will be displayed.

Part II

Spreadsheet Operations

You will find all the commands that relate to the Quattro Pro spreadsheet in this section of the book. Each command resides on one of the pull-down menus that you access either from the keyboard or with your mouse (see Part I).

Many of the commands work on a *block* of cells, which can be either a single cell or a contiguous group of cells. Commands such as Print–Block, Edit–Erase Block, and Edit–Copy prompt you to specify a block of cells which the command will effect. You define a multi-cell block by referring to any opposing pair of corner cells, such as B5..F10. Generally, the upper-left and lower-right cells are used. You have several different methods available for selecting a block.

To Define a Block from the Keyboard

1. Select the Quattro Pro command you want, which will prompt you to specify a block; the mode indicator will display Point.

2. Type the block address (such as **A5** or **D40..M55**), its block name (such as **YEAREND**), or press F3 and select a block name from the list.

3. Press ↵ when finished, and the command will continue.

To Highlight a Block from the Keyboard

1. Select the Quattro Pro command you want, which will prompt you to specify a block; the mode indicator will display Point.

2. Move the cell selector to a corner cell of the block you wish to use. Note that some commands, such as Edit–Copy and Edit–Move, offer you a default block starting and ending at the cursor's location, such as B4..B4. In order to define a block at a different address, you must first press Escape or Backspace.

3. Press the period key once to anchor the corner of the block at this cell.

4. Using the cursor-control keys, move the cell selector to highlight the block.

5. Press ↵ when finished and the command will continue.

To Highlight a Block with Your Mouse

1. Select the Quattro Pro command you want, which will prompt you to specify a block; the mode indicator will display Point.

2. Move the mouse pointer to a corner cell of the block you wish to use.

3. Press and hold down the mouse button to anchor the corner of the block at this cell.

4. Drag the mouse pointer to highlight the block.

5. Press ↵ when finished and the command will continue.

To Highlight a Block Before You Invoke a Command

1. With a mouse, simply drag the mouse pointer over the block to highlight it.

2. From the keyboard, press Shift-F7, the Select key. You will see the Ext indicator on the status line. Using the cursor-control keys, move the cell selector to highlight the block.

3. Once the block is highlighted, invoke the command, which will then act on the highlighted block.

When you are pointing to a block, you can expand the highlight either to the right or down from the anchor cell. The corner of the highlight that you are moving is called the *active* corner.

You can rotate the active corner to another corner of the highlight by pressing the period key. Each press will move the the active corner to the next corner in a clockwise rotation.

You can unanchor a highlighted block by pressing either Escape or Backspace. When you press Escape, the cell selector remains at the corner that had been the anchor cell. Pressing Backspace unanchors the block and returns the cell selector to the cell on which it resided before you issued the command.

To Reference a Block in Another Spreadsheet

You can specify a block in another spreadsheet, or even in a database file, by using Quattro Pro linking syntax. Enclose the file name in square brackets and specify the drive and path when necessary, such as

(C:\DATA\MYFILE)G50..P125

16 Spreadsheet Operations

Note that it is best to have a block name defining the data block in the other spreadsheet, so that you can reference it in the Block command to ensure that you are using the correct data.

DATABASE–DATA ENTRY

With the Database–Data Entry command, you can specify the type of data that will be accepted into the cells in a block. You can have Quattro Pro change any entry to text, or you can have it limit the entries to only valid dates.

To Specify How Data May Be Entered into a Cell

1. From the Ready mode, select **Database** and then **Data Entry**.
2. Choose either **Dates Only**, **General**, or **Labels Only** from the menu.
3. Specify the block of cells.

- **OPTIONS**

    Dates Only: Allows only entries that look like a valid Quattro Pro date.

    General: Resets the block to the default mode, and allows any data to be entered.

    Labels Only: Allows label entries only and changes any numeric entries in the specified block to labels, as though you preceded each entry with a label prefix.

- **NOTES** Keep in mind that the two format options work in different ways. Labels Only automatically converts each entry in the specified block to a label, obviating the need to precede each entry with a label prefix (see Style–Alignment), but Dates Only simply rejects any entry that does not fit one of the Quattro Pro date formats:

- 01-Jan-92
- 01-Jan
- Jan-92
- 01/01/92
- 01/01

See Also Options–Formats–Align Labels, Style–Alignment, Style–Numeric Format

DATABASE–PARADOX ACCESS

The settings on the Database–Paradox Access menu control the switch between Quattro Pro and Paradox when you are running the two at the same time via the Paradox Access.

To Switch to the Paradox Database Program

1. From the Ready mode, select **Database** and then **Paradox Access**.
2. Choose either **Autoload** or **Load File** from the Paradox Access menu to adjust the Paradox Access settings, or select **Go** (Crtl-F10) to enter Paradox.

• OPTIONS

- Autoload: By default, this is set to Yes, so that Quattro Pro will load the file named in the Load File setting each time you switch to it from Paradox. The file will replace the current spreadsheet if you haven't saved it; otherwise, a new spreadsheet window will be opened. Choose No if you do not want the file loaded when you switch to Quattro Pro.

- Go: Switches to Paradox, which will be in the same state as it was when you previously switched to Quattro Pro.
- Load File: Enter the name and, optionally, the location of the file that Quattro Pro should load whenever you switch to it from Paradox. The default is ANSWER.DB, the Paradox answer table.

• **NOTES**   In order to take advantage of the Paradox Access, you must be running Paradox version 3.5 or later on a computer with an 80286 or higher processor and at least two megabytes of RAM. The best way to run the Paradox Access for most computer systems is by starting Paradox with the batch file named PXACCESS.BAT that comes with Quattro Pro.

When a Paradox table is loaded into Quattro Pro, you can't save the file under its original name and location, as that would be a file-sharing violation between the two programs. You can, however, save the data under a new name or location, or as a file type other than Paradox.

See Also   Options–Other–Paradox

DATABASE–QUERY

Use the commands on the Database–Query menu to locate specific information in a block that matches criteria that you specify. Figure II.1 shows the layout for a simple database in Quattro Pro.

ASSIGN NAMES

The Assign Names command creates a block name for each cell in the first record of the data block. It uses the names found in the column titles above them, and is similar to the Edit–Names–Labels command.

Database–Query   19

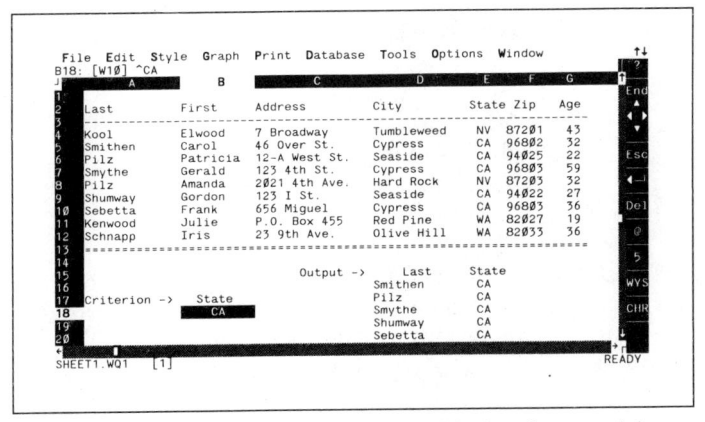

```
    File  Edit  Style  Graph  Print  Database  Tools  Options  Window
B18: [W10] ^CA
        A           B            C              D           E     F     G
 1  Last         First        Address        City         State Zip   Age
 2  ----------------------------------------------------------------------
 3  Kool         Elwood       7 Broadway     Tumbleweed   NV    87201 43
 4  Smithen      Carol        46 Over St.    Cypress      CA    96802 32
 5  Pilz         Patricia     12-A West St.  Seaside      CA    94025 22
 6  Smythe       Gerald       123 4th St.    Cypress      CA    96803 59
 7  Pilz         Amanda       2021 4th Ave.  Hard Rock    NV    87203 32
 8  Shumway      Gordon       123 I St.      Seaside      CA    94022 27
 9  Sebetta      Frank        656 Miguel     Cypress      CA    96803 36
10  Kenwood      Julie        P.O. Box 455   Red Pine     WA    82027 19
11  Schnapp      Iris         23 9th Ave.    Olive Hill   WA    82033 36
12
13
14                                 Output ->   Last        State
15                                             Smithen     CA
16                                             Pilz        CA
17  Criterion ->  State                        Smythe      CA
18                  CA                         Shumway     CA
19                                             Sebetta     CA
20
SHEET1.WQ1  [1]                                                      READY
```

Figure II.1: The data, criteria, and output blocks of a spreadsheet database

To Assign Block Names to the Data Block Columns

1. First, you should have already defined the database block using Database–Query–Block; its first row should contain unique column titles.

2. From the Ready mode, select **Database**, then **Query**, and then **Assign Names**.

• **CAUTION** If the Assign Names command creates a block name that already exists in the spreadsheet, the new definition will overwrite the previous one. There is no warning that this will happen.

See Also   Edit–Names

BLOCK

This command defines the block of data that will serve as the source for the Query commands Assign Names, Delete, Extract, Locate, and Unique. Be sure that the first row of this block contains a unique column title in each column.

To Define the Data Block

1. From the Ready mode, select **Database**, then **Query**, and then **Block**.
2. Specify the block that will serve as the data for the Query commands. Be sure to include the column titles as the first row in the block.

• **NOTES** To specify a database file, such as Paradox or dBASE, as the data block, be sure to include the file name extension. Since there are no cell addresses in a database file, simply refer to any valid block, such as A1..A2, to complete the definition.

CRITERIA TABLE

In order to locate specific records in your data block, you use the Database–Query–Criteria Table command to define the block that contains your search criteria.

To Define the Block for the Criteria Table

1. From the Ready mode, select **Database**, then **Query**, and then **Criteria Table**.
2. Specify the block that will serve as the criteria table for the Query commands.

• **NOTES** The criteria block can be as small as two cells in a column. The first cell must contain a copy of a column title from the data block; the cell below contains the search criterion. The table can include as many columns and rows as are available in the spreadsheet. The criteria you write will always find the same records, whether for the Delete, Extract, Locate, or Unique command.

There are two types of criteria you can write: character and logical formula. You can mix the two types in a multicolumn criteria table, and both can perform many of the same searches. In general, a logical formula criterion can perform more powerful and complex searches than a character criterion.

You can use two types of criteria for searches: character and logical. Character criteria searches locate records that contain the same text as that entered in a criteria table cell. In the criteria table in Figure II.1, the character criterion CA matches all records in which the entry under State is CA. You can use the ? and * wildcards to represent any one character or any several characters, respectively. You can also preface a character criterion with a tilde (~) to search for all characters *except* those specified.

Logical formula criteria, on the other hand, use relational operators to define wider search parameters, such as all people who are older than 30 or whose last name begins with a letter following M in the alphabet. For example, to search for all people in Figure II.1 whose Age is greater than 30, you would enter the search formula +G3>30.

Two rules apply to the use of logical criteria formulas:

- The column title you use in the first row of the criteria table must be the one that is found in the data block.

- The formula should generally refer to a cell in the first row in the column you wish to use to select the records.

In character criteria searches, the column title of the criteria table must be the same as the title of the column in the data block in which the search will be made. In logical criteria searches, the column title of the criteria table can be any valid title from the data block.

Multiple Criteria: Quattro Pro allows two forms of multiple criteria (logical or character) in database searches. By placing all criteria on the same row, you search for all records that meet the first test *and* the second (and so on); by placing criteria on separate rows, you search for records that meet one test *or* the other.

With logical criteria, it's often easier and neater to use a compound logical formula, using the logical operators #AND# and #OR#. To find those who are 32 and live in CA, you could use the formula

+G3=32#AND#D3="CA"

DELETE

You can eliminate all records that are selected by your criteria with the Database–Query–Delete command.

To Delete Matching Records from the Database

1. From the Ready mode, select **Database**, then **Query**, and then **Delete**. You will be offered a menu with the choices Cancel and Delete.

2. Choose **Cancel** to cancel this potentially data-destroying command; or choose **Delete** to continue and delete all records from the database that are selected by the criteria.

- **CAUTION** Before you proceed with the Database–Query–Delete command, use Database–Query–Locate to be absolutely certain that your criteria select only those records that you want to delete. The Edit–Undo command (Alt-F5) will reverse an accidental deletion, but only if you notice the mistake before you make any other changes to the spreadsheet.

If the data block is named by a block name, the cell address of the name does not contract with the data block when records are deleted—its coordinates remain unchanged. Keep this in mind because it could create problems for you the next time you perform database operations using the block name for the data block.

See Also   Database–Query–Block, Database–Query–Criteria Table

EXTRACT

Once you have defined the data block, output block, and criteria table of your database, you can invoke the Database–Query–Extract command to copy selected records in your data to the output block.

To Extract Records to the Output Block

- From the Ready mode, select **Database**, then **Query**, and then **Extract**.

Any records found in the data block by the criteria will be copied to the output block. If there are no matching records, Quattro Pro will issue a beep, and the Database–Query menu will still be active.

- **NOTES** The data that ends up in the output block is a copy of the data in the data block. Only the results of any formulas, not the formulas themselves, appear in the output block. A cell's attributes, such as numeric format, alignment, font, and shading, are copied along with the cell contents. However, a cell's protection status will be ignored, as will any line drawing. The Extract command copies only those fields that are represented in the output block.

- **CAUTION** Any data already in the output block will be erased, whether or not any matching records are found. If you have not yet tested the accuracy of your criteria, it is often beneficial to invoke the Locate command before you use the Extract command.

See Also Database–Query–Block, Database–Query–Output Block

LOCATE

Once you have defined the data block and criteria table of your database, you can search for matching records in your data with the Database–Query–Locate command.

To Locate Records in Your Database

- From the Ready mode, select **Database**, then **Query**, and then **Locate**.

If there are no matching records to be found in the data block, Quattro Pro will issue a beep, and the Database–Query menu will still be active.

- **OPTIONS** The cursor will jump to the first matching record in the data block, and will expand to the full width of the block, completely highlighting the current record. You can do any of the following:

  - Press ↑ to move to the next matching record.

- Press ↓ to move to the previous matching record.
- Press End or Home to jump to the very last or first record in the database, respectively, whether it matches the criteria or not.
- Press → or ← to move between the columns of the currently selected record. This allows you to view the contents of each cell, and also to scroll the screen to view cells that would otherwise not be visible.
- Type a new entry into a cell.
- Press F2 to edit the contents of the current cell.
- Press Escape or ↵ to cancel the operation. The cell selector will return to the cell it was on before you invoked the Locate command.
- Press F7 to return to Ready mode but leave the cell selector on the selected record.

See Also   Database–Query–Block, Database–Query–Criteria Table, Database–Query–Output Block, Edit–Search & Replace

OUTPUT BLOCK

In order to use the Extract or Unique command, you must first define the database output block. The first row of this block must contain copies of one or more column titles from the database block. In Figure II.1, the output block titles are in cells D15 and E15.

To Define the Output Block

1. From the Ready mode, select **Database**, then **Query**, and then **Output Block**.
2. Specify the block that will serve as the output area for the Database–Query–Extract and Unique commands. The first row of this block must include copies of one or more column titles in the data block.

- **NOTES** The output block can contain more than one column, each titled with a copy of a column title from the data block. Their order does not have to match that of columns in the data block.

It is always best to use the Edit–Copy command to copy the necessary data block titles to the output block, so that the titles will match exactly.

In Figure II.1, the output block has just two columns, labeled Last and State. For each record that matched the criteria (State equals CA), only the data from those two fields was copied to the output block.

When defining the output block, you can either limit the number of rows in it or let Quattro Pro use as many rows as necessary by specifying a one-row output block that contains only the column titles. Quattro Pro will then use all the rows below those titles to the bottom of the spreadsheet, if necessary.

- **CAUTION** When you invoke the Extract or Unique command, any data already in the output block will be erased, even if no records are found during the query. If you define a one-row output block, all data from that row to the bottom of the spreadsheet will be erased.

RESET

When you want to work with a different database, criteria table, and output block, use the Database–Query–Reset command to reset all the query settings to their defaults. This will ensure that you start fresh when you define the set of new database operations.

To Reset All Database–Query Settings

- From the Ready mode, select **Database**, then **Query**, and then **Reset**.

UNIQUE

To extract only one copy of multiple matching records, use the Database–Query–Unique command. It behaves just like the Extract command, except that each item that ends up in the output block will be different from all the others. You could use this command to create a list of unique states in the name and address list in Figure II.1.

To Extract Only Unique Records

- From the Ready mode, select **Database**, then **Query**, and then **Unique**.

Any matching records in the data block will be copied to the output block. If there are no matching records to be found, Quattro Pro will issue a beep, and the Database–Query menu will remain active.

- **NOTES** The uniqueness of each record is determined by the column titles represented in the output block. Using the database in Figure II.1, if the output block contained only the State column, then two records would be considered unique only if they each had a different entry in the State column. If you changed the output titles to include both the City and State columns, the uniqueness of each record would be based on the entries in both of those fields. By broadening the scope in this way, more records would be copied to the output block, but each would be different from the others.

- **CAUTION** Just as with the Database–Query–Extract command, any data already in the output block will be erased when you invoke the Unique command.

See Also Database–Query–Block, Database–Query–Criteria Table, Database–Query–Output Block

DATABASE–RESTRICT INPUT

You can invoke the Database–Restrict Input command to have the cell selector move only to unprotected cells within a block you specify. Protected cells will be off-limits.

To Restrict Input to Unprotected Cells

1. Before using this command, there must be unprotected cells in the block.

2. From the Ready mode, select **Database** and then **Restrict Input**.

3. Specify the block in which you want to restrict the cursor. The mode indicator will change to Input, and cursor movement will be restricted to the unprotected cells in the block.

4. You can cancel the restricted access by pressing Escape or ↵.

- **NOTES** This command will function whether or not global protection has been enabled with the Options–Protection command. You can move the cursor only to unprotected cells in the block you have specified, using either the arrow keys or the mouse.

You can enter or edit data in any of the unprotected cells in the block, and press to complete the entry. If you press from the Input mode, however, you will cancel the Restrict Input operation.

See Also Options–Protection, Style–Protection

DATABASE–SORT

You can use the Database–Sort command to sort the rows of a block; this is frequently valuable when a block is also being used as a database.

To Sort the Rows in a Block

1. From the Ready mode, select **Database** and then **Sort**.

2. Select **Block** and then specify the block of cells you wish to sort.

3. Select **1st Key**, and specify the column by which you want to determine the sort order.

28 Spreadsheet Operations

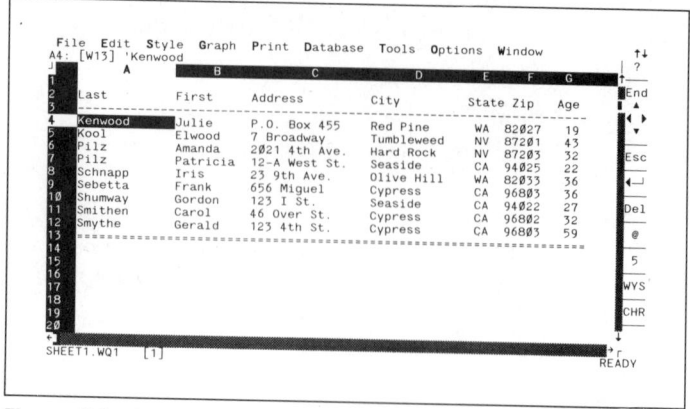

```
  File  Edit  Style  Graph  Print  Database  Tools  Options  Window
A4: [W13] 'Kenwood
        A              B            C                D            E     F      G
 1
 2  Last           First        Address          City         State Zip    Age
 3  ================================================================================
 4  Kenwood        Julie        P.O. Box 455     Red Pine     WA    82027  19
 5  Kool           Elwood       7 Broadway       Tumbleweed   NV    87201  43
 6  Pilz           Amanda       2021 4th Ave.    Hard Rock    NV    87203  32
 7  Pilz           Patricia     12-A West St.    Seaside      CA    94025  22
 8  Schnapp        Iris         23 9th Ave.      Olive Hill   WA    82033  36
 9  Sebetta        Frank        656 Miguel       Cypress      CA    96803  36
10  Shumway        Gordon       123 I St.        Seaside      CA    94022  27
11  Smithen        Carol        46 Over St.      Cypress      CA    96802  32
12  Smythe         Gerald       123 4th St.      Cypress      CA    96803  59
13  ================================================================================

SHEET1.WQ1   [1]                                                          READY
```

Figure II.2: Sorting the block A4..G12 by last name and first name

4. Select **A** to sort in ascending order (A–Z), or select **D** to sort in descending order (Z–A).

5. You can then select **2nd Key** (and on up through 5th Key) to choose a column to use as a second sort key, which will break any ties in the 1st Key column.

6. Select **Go** to sort the block.

• **EXAMPLE** The database block shown in Figure II.2 was sorted with the last name column, Last, as the 1st Key option. The first name column, First, was used for the 2nd Key option. To perform that sort:

1. From the Ready mode, select **Database**, then **Sort**, and then **Reset** to reset all the sort options to their defaults.

2. Select **Block**, and specify the block A4..G12 as the block to be sorted. Do not leave out any columns, and do not include the rows with the column titles or dashed lines.

3. Select **1st Key**, and choose cell A4 in the last name column, and press . (It does not matter which row you specify, as long as it is a valid address in the column you want.)

4. You will be prompted for the sort order; choose A for ascending order (A–Z).

5. Select **2nd Key**, and choose cell B4 in the first name column, and press ↵.

6. You will again be prompted for the sort order; choose **A** for ascending order.

7. Select **Go** to sort the block.

Notice that the sort order for the two identical entries in the last name column in Figure II.2 was determined by their entries in the first name column.

• **NOTES** When a row is rearranged during a sort, a formula in that row will adjust its relative cell references to its new location after sorting, just as it would if it were copied there with the Edit–Copy command. (Absolute cell references, of course, will not adjust.)

If the formula was referring to another cell in its own row, there will be no change in its result after sorting—it will still be referring to the same data. However, if the formula was referring to a cell outside of its own row, its result will very likely be different after the sort, because it will have adjusted its reference and will be referring to a different cell.

SORT RULES

Use the Database–Sort–Sort Rules option to modify the rules by which Quattro Pro sorts a block.

- **Numbers before Labels:** When sorting in ascending order, Quattro Pro places text entries before numeric ones, so that the word *zebra* would be placed above the number *1*. Choose Yes and any numbers will be sorted before text.

- **Label Order:** By default, the sorting sequence is in ASCII order and is therefore case-sensitive: uppercase letters (*A, B, C*) come before lowercase ones (*a, b, c*). Choose Dictionary to sort without regard to case: The name *alan* will come before *Xavier*.

• **NOTES** You can also modify the sort rules by using the Options–International–Use Sort Table command.

Spreadsheet Operations

- **CAUTION** When you are defining the block to be sorted, don't mistakenly include any rows or columns that you do not want sorted into the block, such as column titles, dashed dividing rows, or totals. On the other hand, be absolutely certain that you include all the columns associated with the data you are sorting. If you neglect one or more columns on either side of the block, your data will be sorted into disaster, since only part of each row will be included in the sort.

See Also   Database–Query–Block,   Options–International–Use Sort Table

EDIT–COPY

With the Edit–Copy command (Ctrl-C), you can copy the contents and formatting of one block (the source) to another block (the destination). As in all Quattro Pro commands, the block can be a single cell or a contiguous rectangle of cells.

To Copy a Block

1. From the Ready mode, select **Edit**, then **Copy** (Ctrl-C).
2. Specify the source block and press ↵.
3. Specify the target block and press ↵.

- **NOTES**   See the introduction to Part II for information on specifying source and target bolcks.

When a cell is copied, its contents and all the attributes associated with the cell are copied to the target location, including the cell's numeric format, font, line drawing, cell shading, alignment, and protection status. The target cell will therefore be an exact duplicate of the source cell. See "Referencing Cell Addresses" in Part V for a discussion of formula references in cells that you copy.

- **OPTIONS**   There are four possible combinations when copying a block. You can copy one cell to another cell, one cell to a block, a block to a single cell, and a block to another block.

The simplest operation is that of copying a single cell to another cell. To copy one cell to a block, you need only specify the block as the destination, and the source cell will be duplicated in all the cells of the block. When you copy a block to a single cell, the block will be duplicated starting with the destination cell as its upper-left corner cell.

In order to copy a block to another block, remember this rule: copy a single column to a single row, or a single row to a single column.

- **CAUTION**   You should exercise caution when using the Edit–Copy command, since any information already in the destination cells will be overwritten.

See Also   Edit–Move, Edit–Names, Edit–Transpose, Edit–Values

EDIT–DELETE

The Edit–Delete command allows you to delete rows or columns from the spreadsheet. The operation is the same for both rows and columns.

To Delete Rows or Columns

1. From the Ready mode, choose **Edit**, then **Delete**.
2. Select either **Rows** or **Columns**.
3. Specify the rows or columns you wish to delete and press ↵.

- **NOTES**   When you specify the columns or rows that you wish to delete, you must define a valid block reference—any block that includes those columns or rows. When you delete one or more columns (or rows) by using the Edit–Delete command, the columns to the right (or the rows below) are all moved to the left (or up) to fill the resulting gap. Any formula cell references affected by the deletion will be adjusted accordingly.

• **CAUTION**   Accidentally deleting rows or columns can be a disaster, so exercise care when using the Edit–Delete command (see also the Edit–Undo command). You can also destroy formulas that reference cells in a deleted row or column. When a formula refers to a cell whose row or column is deleted, the formula's reference will change to ERR. You would have to revise the formula to correct or remove the invalid cell reference.

See Also   Edit–Insert, Edit–Move, Edit–Undo

EDIT–ERASE BLOCK

You use the Edit–Erase Block command (Ctrl-E) to erase the contents of a cell or block. You can also use the Del key to erase the current cell or selected block.

To Erase a Block with the Command

1. From the Ready mode, select **Edit**, and then **Erase Block** (Ctrl-E).
2. Specify the block you wish to erase and press ↵.

• **NOTES**   The Edit–Erase Block command erases only the contents of a cell. It does not affect any of the formatting attributes attached to the cell. To clear a cell of all formatting, you must invoke each of the formatting commands and select the appropriate reset option.

- **CAUTION** There are several ways to protect yourself from losing data due to an accidental erasure with the Edit–Erase Block command:

  - Use the Edit–Undo command immediately after erasing (so long as you have enabled it with the Options–Other–Undo command).

  - If you neglect to use the Edit–Undo command, you can still use the Tools–Macro–Transcript command to rebuild the spreadsheet.

  - Leave protected those cells that you don't want erased (or use the Style–Protection command to protect cells that were unprotected), and enable protection with the Options–Protection command.

  - Frequently save your worksheet to disk so you can retrieve it in case of problems.

See Also Edit–Delete, Edit–Undo, Style–Protection

EDIT–FILL

The Edit–Fill command makes it easy for you to fill a block of cells with consecutive numbers.

To Fill a Block of Cells with Consecutive Numbers

1. From the Ready mode, select **Edit** and then **Fill**.

2. Specify the destination block (the cells to be filled) and press ↵.

3. Enter the start value (the number from which to begin incrementing), and press ↵.

4. Enter the step value (the number by which to increase each cell), and press ↵.

34 Spreadsheet Operations

5. Enter the stop value (the number at which to stop incrementing), and press ↵.

• **NOTES**   Your entries for the start, step, and stop values can be numbers, formulas, or addresses of cells that contain values. The numbers that the command places in the destination block will always be values, not formulas. The block is filled column by column. You can have the block filled in descending order by specifying a negative step value. In that case, be sure that the stop value is smaller than the start value.

There are two ways to limit the size of the destination block. You can specify the exact size of the block and a stop value that is large enough not to limit the fill block, or you can specify a stop value that will precisely limit the destination block's size.

• **CAUTION**   Data already in the fill block will be overwritten.

EDIT–INSERT

Use the Edit–Insert command to insert new rows or columns into the spreadsheet. The operation is the same for both rows and columns.

To Insert Rows or Columns

1. From the Ready mode, select **Edit**, and then **Insert**.

2. Select either **Rows** or **Columns**.

3. Specify the block size of the rows or columns you wish to insert and press ↵.

• **NOTES**   Just as with the Edit–Delete command, you must indicate the number of rows or columns to insert by specifying a valid block reference. The new rows or columns will be inserted at the beginning of the block you specify. If you specify the block A6..A9 for the Edit–Insert–Rows command, four new rows will be inserted at row 6. What had been row 6 will now be row 10.

When you insert one or more columns (or rows) by using the Edit–Insert command, the columns to the right (or the rows below) are all moved to the right (or down) to make room for the new columns or rows. If there is already an entry in the last column (or row) of the spreadsheet, you will not be allowed to insert a new column (or row). Any formula cell references affected by an insertion will be adjusted accordingly. If a formula refers to cell F10 and you insert three new rows at row 8, the contents of rows 8 and below will be moved down three rows, and the formula will adjust to reference cell F13.

See Also   Edit–Delete

EDIT–MOVE

With the Edit–Move command (Ctrl-M), you can move the contents and formatting of one block (the source) to another block (the destination). As in all Quattro Pro commands, the block can be a single cell or a contiguous rectangle of cells.

To Move a Block

1. From the Ready mode, select **Edit**, and then **Move** (Ctrl-M).
2. Specify the source block and press ↵.
3. Specify the target block and press ↵.

• **NOTES**   For information on specifying the source and target blocks, see the introduction to Part II. When you move a cell, its contents and all the attributes associated with it are moved to the target location, including the cell's numeric format, font, line drawing, cell shading, alignment, and protection status. The target cell will therefore be an exact duplicate of what had been in the source cell.

Unlike the effects of the Edit–Copy command, cell references within a formula do not adjust when the formula is moved. A formula that refers to cell B5 will still refer to B5, no matter where you might move that formula. On the other hand, no matter what the contents of the source cell may be, any formulas in the spreadsheet that refer to it will follow that cell when it is moved.

• **CAUTION** Moving one cell onto another can have the same potentially disastrous results that can occur with the Edit–Delete command. If you move a cell onto cell K20, any formulas that had referenced K20 will now display ERR; you have effectively deleted that cell.

See Also Edit–Copy, Edit–Delete

EDIT–NAMES

The commands on the Edit–Names menu include Create, Delete, Labels, Reset, and Make Table. They give you access to block names, an often under-utilized feature in Quattro Pro. You can assign a block name of up to 15 characters to any block in the spreadsheet. Once you have named a block, you can use the name, instead of the actual cell addresses, in any Quattro Pro command or formula.

When a Quattro Pro command, such as Print–Block, prompts you for a block address, you can specify a block name instead of the cell coordinates. Instead of typing the name, you can press the Choices key, F3, and select the name from the list of all block names in the spreadsheet.

CREATE

The Edit–Names–Create command creates a new block name or revises an existing name.

To Name a Block with the Create Command

1. From the Ready mode, select **Edit**, then **Names**, and then **Create**. A list will be displayed showing all existing block names in the spreadsheet.

2. Enter a new block name of up to 15 characters, or select an existing name from the list to change the block address to which the name refers.

3. Press ↵, and you will be prompted for the block that the name should define.

4. Specify a block in the spreadsheet and press ↵.

DELETE

The Edit–Names–Delete command lets you remove a block name from the block names list (F3).

To Delete a Block Name

1. From the Ready mode, select **Edit**, then **Names**, and then **Delete**.

2. Select the name you wish to delete from the list of block names, or type in the name that you wish to delete.

3. Press and the name will be deleted from the spreadsheet.

* **NOTES**   When you delete a block name, the name is simply removed from the internal list of block names, and will no longer be available. The block of cells that the name defined is in no way affected, although formulas that once referred to the block name will now refer to the actual cell coordinates that the name defined.

LABELS

The Edit–Names–Label command lets you assign multiple single-cell block names from text labels in the spreadsheet. You must first create the text entries in the spreadsheet, spelling them exactly as you want the names to appear. When you invoke the command, you choose whether you want these text entries to name the cells to their right or left, or above or below them.

This command also offers a quick single-step way to assign many block names. It ensures accuracy because the spelling for each name is based on spreadsheet labels that you have already entered.

To Name a Block with the Labels Command

1. From the Ready mode, select **Edit**, then **Names**, and then **Labels**.
2. Choose **Right**, **Down**, **Left**, or **Up**, depending on the location of the location of the cells to be named in relation to the spreadsheet labels.
3. Specify the block that contains the labels.
4. Press ↵, and the names will be created.

• **CAUTION** Be sure the labels you create are spelled exactly as you want the block names to appear. Don't leave stray spaces before or after the labels, or the names will include those spaces. Don't use numbers, as the command requires text entries. All text entries in the block will be used, so avoid unnecessary entries in any of the other cells, or names will be created for them as well.

RESET

The Edit–Names–Reset command clears all block names from the spreadsheet.

To Remove All Block Names

1. From the Ready mode, select **Edit**, then **Names**, and then **Reset**.
2. Choose **Yes** to delete all the block names from the spreadsheet, or **No** to cancel the command.

• **CAUTION** Because this command deletes every block name in the spreadsheet, you should use care not to invoke it accidentally.

If you invoke the Edit–Undo command immediately after deleting all block names, the names will be restored. (See the Edit–Undo command.)

MAKE TABLES

The Edit–Names–Make Table command creates a two-column list in the spreadsheet of all block names and their cell coordinates. The list can be quite helpful, such as in documenting the spreadsheet, finding duplicate names for the same block, or finding names that only refer to ERR.

To Create a List of Block Names

- From the Ready mode, select the Edit–Names–Make Table command. You will be prompted for the block in which the table will be created. Specify the upper-left cell of the two-column block and press ↵.

• **CAUTION** The table will overwrite any data in the cells in which it is created. If the addresses of the block names change as you modify the spreadsheet, you will have to invoke the Make Table command again in order to have an updated list.

See Also Database–Query–Assign Names, Tools–Macro–Name

EDIT–SEARCH & REPLACE

The Edit–Search & Replace command offers you a means of searching for specific characters within a block of cells. They can be part of text or value cells, or of formulas.

You can also choose to replace the data for which you are searching with other data that you specify. In this way, the command is very much like a search and replace command in most word processors, although in Quattro Pro it has some very powerful options.

To Search for Data in the Spreadsheet

1. From the Ready mode, start by selecting **Edit**, then **Search & Replace**, and then **Block**.
2. Specify the block you want to include in the search.
3. Choose **Search String**.
4. Type in the characters that you want to find, such as SUM (an @function), C44 (a cell address), 19 (a number), or SOMENAME (a block name), and then press ↵.
5. To begin the search, choose **Next**. To search backward from the cursor's current position, choose **Previous**.

The cursor will jump to the first cell that contains the specified search string. You will be offered a menu of actions, with the prompt *Replace this string?*.

- **Yes** replaces the characters in the cell with your specified Replace String. Note that if there is no entry in Replace String, the characters will be erased from the current cell. The search will continue to look for the next occurrence of the specified Search String.

- **No** leaves the characters untouched, but continues searching for the next occurrence of the specified Search String. If no other cells are found, the cursor will return to the cell on which the search was started.

- **All** replaces the characters in this cell with your specified Replace String, and in all other cells containing characters that match the Search String.

- **Edit** pauses and makes changes to the current cell. When you are finished editing, press and the search will continue.

- **Quit** ends the search; the cursor will remain on the current cell.

● **NOTES** From the Ready mode, you can type Ctrl-N to invoke the Edit–Search & Replace–Next command. The search will use the current settings on the Search & Replace menu. You can also use Ctrl-P to invoke the Previous command.

Don't confuse this command with the Database–Query–Locate command, which can only be used when you have a block of data structured as a database.

• **OPTIONS**   Before you invoke the Next or Previous command, you can fine-tune the search by using the optional settings on the Search & Replace menu.

Replace String   The characters you enter here will replace the characters you specified in Search String, if you choose Yes or All from the menu when a matching cell is found.

Look In   Choose **Formula** from the Look In menu to have the search look at characters in formulas (not at their results). It will also find cells that are not formulas, but contain the desired string.

Choose **Value** to search only the results of formulas. In this case, a cell containing 3+9 would be found if the search string were 12, as would a cell containing the number 12. But a cell containing 12+99 would not be found.

The **Condition** options lets you specify a Search String that is a logical formula, which will serve as a conditional search criterion. For example, entering the formula A1>=100 as the search string will find all cells with a value greater than or equal to 100. You can either use the address of the current cell or a ? to represent the current cell.

Direction   By default, Quattro Pro searches across each row in the block; choose **Column** to search down each column in the block, or **Row** to restore the default if you've changed it.

Match   By default, this option is set to **Part**, so that the Search String will be found even if it is a part of a larger group of characters. To find only separate occurrences of the search string, choose **Whole**.

Case Sensitive   By default, this option is set to **Any Case**, so that your entry in Search String can be any combination of upper- or lowercase letters. The string *Year* would be found whether you entered *YEAR*, *year*, or *Year*. Choose **Exact Case** if you want to match the case exactly.

Options Reset Use the Options Reset command to return all the Search & Replace settings to their defaults.

● **CAUTION** When the search locates a matching cell and offers you the action menu, don't choose All unless you want to replace every matching occurrence. The Edit–Undo command will only undo the last cell replaced; all the others will be irrevocably changed.

See Also   Database–Query

EDIT–TRANSPOSE

The Edit–Transpose command is similar to the Edit–Copy command. The difference is that it transposes the rows and columns of the source block when it copies them into the target block.

To Transpose a Block

1. From the Ready mode, select **Edit**, and then **Transpose**.
2. Specify the source block and press ↵.
3. Specify the target block and press ↵.

See the introduction of Part II for information on specifying source and target blocks.

● **CAUTION** Just as with the Copy command, any formulas in the source block will adjust their relative cell references in the target block when copied with the Transpose command. Generally, their new location in the transposed block will be totally unrelated to their original one, and their results will therefore be irrelevant. For this reason, you will generally transpose data, but not formulas.

See Also   Edit–Copy

EDIT–UNDO

The Edit–Undo command (Alt-F5) cancels your last operation and returns the spreadsheet to its state before that operation. If you make a cell entry that replaces the contents of a cell, invoking the Edit–Undo command will return that cell to its prior condition.

By default, this command is disabled. Before you can use it, you must first enable it with the command Options–Other–Undo–Enable.

To Undo an Operation

- From the Ready mode, select **Edit**, then **Undo** (Alt-F5), and your last operation in the spreadsheet will be reversed.

● **NOTES** The Edit–Undo command will cancel only the most recent spreadsheet operation. It is a toggle command, so pressing it a second time will reinstate that operation. If you want the Undo command available every time you use Quattro Pro, enable it with the Options–Other–Undo–Enable command, and then save the Quattro Pro system settings with the Options–Update command.

● **CAUTION** Some operations can't be undone by this command, such as adding line drawing and cell shading, and deleting a file from disk.

See Also Options–Other–Undo, Tools–Macro–Transcript

EDIT–VALUES

The Edit–Values command is very much like the Edit–Copy command. The difference is that any formulas in the source block will have only their results copied to the target block. This command offers a convenient way to separate the results from formulas, for example, to eliminate unneeded formulas from the spreadsheet.

To Copy Formulas Only as Values

1. From the Ready mode, select the Edit–Values command.
2. Specify the source block and press ↵.
3. Specify the target block and press ↵.

● **NOTES** For information on specifying source and target blocks, see the introduction to Part II.

See Also   Edit–Copy

FILE–CLOSE

Use the Close command on the File menu to close the current window (remove it from the screen and the computer's memory). The window you close may contain a spreadsheet or a File Manager session.

To Close a Window

1. From the Ready mode, select **File** and then **Close**.
2. If you have not modified the current spreadsheet since you last saved it, the current window will be closed and removed from the display.
3. If you have made changes to the spreadsheet but have not saved it, the window will not close. You will instead be offered the prompt *Lose your changes?* along with a menu with the choices No and Yes.
4. To close the window, choose **Yes**, but realize that the changes you made to the spreadsheet will be lost when

the window is closed. *Or,* choose **No** to cancel the command and keep the window open.

5. The program will return to Ready mode.

• **CAUTION**   Use the File–Close command judiciously. Closing a spreadsheet that you have modified but not saved will result in the loss of the changes you have made. You will have to retrieve the file from disk and start over from that point. (Refer to the Tools–Macro–Transcript command to see how to recover from such a disaster.)

See Also   File–Close All, File–Erase, File–Exit, File–Save

FILE–CLOSE ALL

When you have one or more windows open, the File–Close All command lets you remove them all (both from the screen and from the computer's memory) in a single operation. You could achieve the same result by issuing the File–Close command for each open window.

To Close All Open Windows

1. From the Ready mode, select **File** and then **Close All**.

2. If you have not modified any of the open spreadsheets since you last saved them, all of the open windows will be closed and removed from the display and memory. Any spreadsheet that you have modified since you last saved it will not be automatically closed. You will instead be offered the prompt *Lose your changes?* along with a menu with the choices No and Yes.

3. To close that window, choose **Yes**, but realize that the changes you made to that spreadsheet will be lost. *Or,* choose **No** to keep that window open.

4. When you have decided to keep or close each of the modified spreadsheet windows, the program will return to Ready mode.

● **CAUTION** The File–Close All command is potentially even more destructive than the File–Close command, since it affects all open spreadsheets, not just the current one. Always exercise caution when using this command.

See Also   File–Close, File–Erase, File–Exit, File–Save

FILE–DIRECTORY

The File–Directory command lets you change the default disk drive and directory, or *path*, for the current Quattro Pro session.

To Change the Current (Default) Directory

1. From the Ready mode, select **File** and then **Directory**. The current directory will be displayed in a dialog box, such as D:\92TAXES.

2. You can type in a new directory path, which will clear the current directory path from the dialog box. For example, type A:\ to access the floppy disk in your A drive. *Or*, press F2 to edit the current path. When editing an entry, you can use any of the editing keystrokes shown in Table I.1.

3. When you have entered the new path, press ↵.

● **NOTES** This command affects only the current session of Quattro Pro. The next time you run the program, the default directory will be determined by the setting for the Options–Startup–Directory command.

See Also   File–Open, File–Save, File–Save As, Options–Startup–Directory, Tools–Import, Tools–Xtract, Part IV: The File Manager

FILE–ERASE

Use the File–Erase command to erase the contents of the current spreadsheet without removing the spreadsheet and its window from memory. All data are erased and any cell formatting is set back to the default, leaving a blank, unnamed spreadsheet. This is equivalent to issuing the File–Close command, followed by the File–New command.

To Erase the Current Spreadsheet

1. From the Ready mode, select **File** and then **Erase**.

2. If you have not made changes to the current spreadsheet since you last saved it, the spreadsheet contents will be erased. If you have made changes to the spreadsheet but have not saved it, the contents will remain untouched. You will instead be offered the prompt *Lose your changes?* along with a menu with the choices No and Yes.

3. To erase the spreadsheet, choose **Yes**, but realize that the changes you made to it since saving it will be lost. *Or,* choose **No** to cancel the command and leave the spreadsheet untouched.

4. The program will return to Ready mode.

• **CAUTION** Just as with the File–Close and Close–All commands, you will lose data when you issue the File–Erase command in a spreadsheet that has not been saved.

See Also   File–Close, File–New

FILE–EXIT

Use the File–Exit command (Ctrl-X) when you wish to quit from Quattro Pro. The File–Exit command is the only way you should leave Quattro Pro. You should not simply turn off or reboot your computer while Quattro Pro is still running.

To Exit from Quattro Pro

1. From the Ready mode, select **File** and then **Exit** (Ctrl-X).

2. If you have not modified any of the open spreadsheets since you last saved them, the program will end and you will be returned to the DOS prompt or your DOS environment. However, if there are any spreadsheets that you have modified since you last saved them, the program will not terminate. Instead, for each modified spreadsheet, you will be prompted *Lose your changes and Exit?* along with a menu with the choices No, Yes, and Save & Exit.

3. To exit from Quattro Pro without saving the spreadsheet, choose **Yes**, but realize that the changes you have made to it will be lost. To cancel the Exit routine and return to the Ready mode with all spreadsheets still open, choose **No**. To save the spreadsheet to disk and continue with the orderly exit from Quattro Pro, choose **Save & Exit**.

4. When you have completed step 3 for each modified spreadsheet, the program will terminate.

• **CAUTION** Just as with the File–Close and Close–All commands, you can lose data when you issue the File–Exit command and you have not saved one or more spreadsheets. Be sure to save your work if you intend to keep it, and exercise caution as you prepare to exit from Quattro Pro.

See Also   File–Close, File–Close All, File–Utilities–DOS Shell

FILE–NEW

The File–New command creates a new window that contains a blank spreadsheet named SHEET#, where # is the number of new windows you have opened during the current session with Quattro Pro. The new spreadsheet will be the active one.

To Open a New, Blank Spreadsheet

- From the Ready mode, select **File** and then **New**. A new window containing a blank spreadsheet will be opened.

• **NOTES** You can open as many as 32 windows at the same time in Quattro Pro. Creating a new spreadsheet with the File–New command will not affect any spreadsheet windows that are already open.

See Also File–Erase, File–Open, File–Retrieve

FILE–OPEN

Use the File–Open command when you want to work with a spreadsheet that has been saved to a file on your disk. The file will be loaded into a new window and will become the active spreadsheet.

To Open a Spreadsheet in the Current Directory

1. From the Ready mode, select **File** and then **Open**. A dialog box will appear, the input line of which will display the current drive and path, such as D:\TAXES\, as well as the

50 Spreadsheet Operations

file filter *.W??. The box will display a list of all the files and subdirectories in the current directory that have file name extensions that begin with W. An example of the screen is shown in the spreadsheet in Figure II.3.

2. Use the arrow keys to highlight a file in the list, *or* type in a file name that can be found in the current directory.

3. Press ↵ to open that file, *or* with a mouse, simply click on the file you wish to open.

To Open a Spreadsheet from a Different Directory

1. From the Ready mode, select **File** and then **Open**.

2. Highlight a subdirectory name in the list and press , or click on the subdirectory with your mouse, to display the contents of that subdirectory. *Or,* press Escape twice to clear the file filter, drive, and directory from the input line of the dialog box.

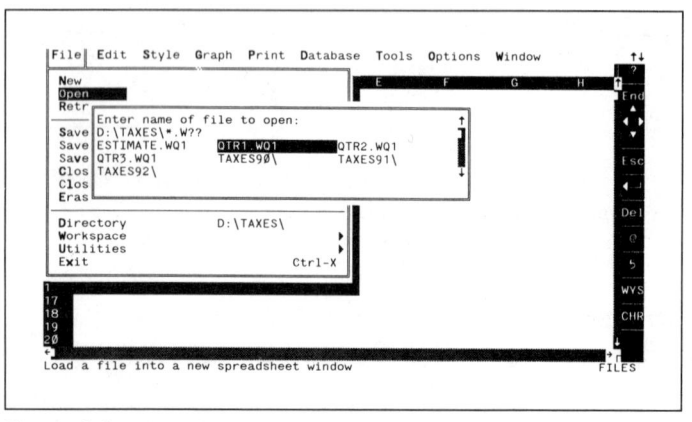

Figure II.3: The File-Open command displays the files and subdirectories in the current directory

3. Type in a new directory and file name and press ↵ to open that file. *Or,* type just the directory such as F:\MYWORK\, and press ↵ to display a list of files and subdirectories in that directory. Select a file from the list as described in the previous section.

To Open a Password-Protected Spreadsheet

1. From the Ready mode, select **File** and then **Open**.

2. Select a file, as described in the preceding sections. If the file is password-protected, you will be prompted to enter the password.

3. Type the password exactly as it was created, being sure to use uppercase and lowercase letters to match the original. If you specify the correct password, the file will be loaded into Quattro Pro. You will also need to know the password when you access a password-protected spreadsheet with the File–Retrieve, File–Workspace, and Tools–Combine commands.

• **NOTES** When the list of files is displayed for the File–Open command (or for any of the other commands that require you to specify a file name), you can manipulate the list in several ways to offer more information:

- Type a new file name filter to display a different list of files. For example, instead of *.W??, you could type *.DB to list all Paradox database files.

- Press the + key to show the date and time each file was modified, as well as the file's size. Press the – key to toggle back to the name-only display.

- Press F3 to expand the list to full-screen size. As you highlight a file in the list, its date, time, and file size appear above the list. Press F3 again to shrink the list back to its original size.

- Press Backspace to display a list of files in the parent directory (the directory above the current directory).

52 Spreadsheet Operations

- To display the files in a subdirectory of the currently displayed directory, just highlight that directory's name in the list and press ↵ (or click on the directory with your mouse).

Quattro Pro can read files from many other programs and load them into a spreadsheet without any intermediate translation. It recognizes a file's format by its file name extension. See the File–Save command for a complete list of file types and their file name extensions.

See Also   File–Directory, File–New, File–Retrieve, File–Workspace, Tools–Combine, Tools–Import, Tools–Update Links, Part IV: File Manager

FILE–RETRIEVE

With the File–Retrieve command, you load a spreadsheet from disk into the current window, replacing the spreadsheet that had been in that window. With this command, a spreadsheet window must already be active, unlike with the File–Open command, which creates a new window for the incoming file.

To Retrieve a Spreadsheet into the Current Window

1. From the Ready mode, select **File** and then **Retrieve**.

2. If you have made changes to the current spreadsheet but have not saved it, you will be prompted *Lose your changes?* along with a menu with the choices No and Yes.

3. To replace the current spreadsheet with one from disk, choose **Yes**, but realize that the changes you made to the spreadsheet will be lost when the other spreadsheet is brought in. Choose **No** to cancel the command and leave the current spreadsheet untouched.

4. If you choose Yes, or have not modified the current spreadsheet since you last saved it, you will be offered a list of files in the current directory. Select a file from the list using one of the selection methods described under the File–Open command.

5. The file will be retrieved into the current window.

- **CAUTION** Unlike the File–Open command, File–Retrieve replaces the current spreadsheet with a spreadsheet from disk. Just as with the File–Close, File–Close All, and File–Erase commands, you will lose data when you retrieve a file into a spreadsheet that has not been saved.

See Also File–Directory, File–New, File–Open, File–Save, File–Workspace, Tools–Combine, Tools–Import, Tools–Update Links

FILE–SAVE

You use the File–Save command (Ctrl-S) to save the current spreadsheet to a file on disk. You should use this command many times in a Quattro Pro session to ensure that your work is safely stored on disk.

To Save a Spreadsheet for the First Time

1. From the Ready mode, select **File** and then **Save** (Ctrl-S).

2. The resulting dialog box prompts you for a name and lists the files in the current directory. To save the spreadsheet in a new file, type a file name that hasn't been used and press ↵. To replace the contents of an existing file, select a name from the list. To save the spreadsheet in a different directory, edit the path and then type or select a file name.

To Save a Spreadsheet that is Already Named

1. From the Ready mode, select **File** and then **Save** (Ctrl-S). Since the file already exists on disk, Quattro Pro will offer a menu with the choices Cancel, Replace, and Backup, and the prompt *File already exists*.

2. To save the current spreadsheet so that it replaces the data in the file on disk, choose **Replace**. To back up the file on disk and save the current spreadsheet to the file, choose **Backup** (see Notes). To cancel the Save operation and return to Ready mode, choose **Cancel**.

To Save a Spreadsheet Under Password-Protection

1. From the Ready mode, select **File**, and then **Save** (or any of the other commands that save your work to disk).

2. When prompted for the file name, type the name followed by a space and the letter **P** (for password), then press ↵.

3. Now type the password (up to 15 characters) at the prompt. You won't see your keystrokes, as Quattro Pro will disguise them to ensure secrecy.

4. Press ↵, and you will be prompted to verify the password by typing it again. Be sure to use uppercase and lowercase letters exactly as you did the first time.

5. Press ↵, and if you typed the password the same way both times, your spreadsheet will be saved.

• **NOTES** When you invoke the File–Save command in a spreadsheet that already exists on disk, Quattro Pro warns you with the choices Cancel, Replace, and Backup that you will be overwriting that file when the current spreadsheet is saved.

When you choose Backup, the spreadsheet file on disk is renamed with an extension of .BAK instead of .WQ1. For example, if the file had been named MOREDATA.WQ1, the Backup procedure would create a file called MOREDATA.BAK. Then, your spreadsheet data in Quattro Pro is saved under the original name, in this case MOREDATA.WQ1. In this way, you will have two versions of your spreadsheet on disk—one named with a .WQ1 extension (the most recent data) and one named with a .BAK extension (the previous version).

In addition to password protection, you also have the option of saving a spreadsheet in a different file format whenever you use the File–Save, File–Save All, File–Save As, or Tools–Xtract command.

When you save a spreadsheet, Quattro Pro automatically appends an extension to the file name. The default for spreadsheet files is .WQ1, but you can specify a different default extension in the Options–Startup–File Extension command.

You can specify any extension for a file name, but certain extensions are a signal to Quattro Pro to write the file in a specific format (the internal structure of the data). When you want to save a file in a different format, all you have to do is apply the appropriate extension. Table II.1 shows all the available extensions and their associated file formats.

See Also   File–Directory, File–Open, File–Save All, File–Save As, File–Utilities–SQZ!, File–Workspace, Tools–Xtract

FILE–SAVE ALL
Version 3 Only

In Quattro Pro 3, to save every open spreadsheet to disk in one operation, use the File–Save All command. This is equivalent to issuing the File–Save command for each open spreadsheet.

To Save All Open Spreadsheets

1. From the Ready mode, select **File** and then **Save All**.
2. Each file will be saved to disk, one after the other, as though you had issued the File–Save command for each

Table II.1: Available Extensions and File Formats.

Extension	Format
DB	Paradox
DB2	dBASE II
DBF	dBASE III, III PLUS, and IV
DIF	VisiCalc
RXD	Reflex Release 1
R2D	Reflex Release 2
SLK	Multiplan
WKS	Lotus 1-2-3 Release 1A
WK1	Lotus 1-2-3 Releases 2.01 and 2.2
WK3	Lotus 1-2-3, Release 3 (within 1-2-3 Release 3, save your spreadsheet with a .WK1 extension)
WKE	Lotus 1-2-3 Academic Edition
WRK	Symphony Release 1.2
WR1	Symphony Release 2.0
WKQ	Quattro 1
WQ1	Quattro Pro
WKP	Surpass
WK$	Lotus 1-2-3 Release 1A, compressed with SQZ!
WK!	Lotus 1-2-3 Release 2.01 and 2.2, compressed with SQZ!
WR$	Symphony Release 1.2, compressed with SQZ!
WR!	Symphony Release 2.0, compressed with SQZ!
WKZ	Quattro 1, compressed with SQZ!
WQ!	Quattro Pro, compressed with SQZ!

spreadsheet. After the save routine has been run for each spreadsheet, Quattro Pro will return to the Ready mode.

● **NOTES** See the File–Save command for the procedure for saving a single file. If you choose Cancel for one of the spreadsheet windows during the Save All routine, that spreadsheet won't be saved; however, the command will not be canceled and will continue with the next open spreadsheet.

If a spreadsheet has not yet been named, you can password-protect it using the procedure shown under File–Save.

See Also File–Directory, File–Save, File–Save As, File–Workspace, Tools–Xtract

FILE–SAVE AS

The File–Save As command lets you save the current spreadsheet under a new name.

To Save a Spreadsheet Under a New Name

1. From the Ready mode, select **File**, and then **Save As**. The current spreadsheet's drive, directory, and file name will be displayed, such as D:\DATA\MYDATA.WQ1.

2. Press F2 to edit the path, file name, or extension. You would do this if, for example, you wanted to save the file MYDATA.WQ1 under the name MYDATA2.WQ1. While editing an entry, you can use any of the keystrokes listed in Table I.1. Or you can type a completely new file name (and, optionally, a new path) to replace the current one. You can Press Escape to clear the file name but display a list of all spreadsheet files in the current directory. You can then select a name from the list.

3. When you have entered the new name, press ↵ to save the spreadsheet and return to Ready mode.

- **NOTES** If the new name you create already exists on disk, you will be offered the Cancel, Replace, and Backup menu to warn you that you will be overwriting an existing file. You can also specify a password when you save the spreadsheet. See the File–Save command for more on these procedures.

Remember that you can press Escape at any time to cancel the current command, or Ctrl-Break to return immediately to the Ready mode.

See Also File–Directory, File–Save, File–Save All, File–Workspace, Tools–Xtract

FILE–UTILITIES

DOS SHELL

With the File–Utilities–DOS Shell command in Quattro Pro 3, you can run another program, DOS command, or batch file while Quattro Pro and all of its open windows remain in memory. When the other program is finished, control returns automatically to Quattro Pro. You can also choose to go to the DOS prompt, which is the only option in Quattro Pro versions 1 and 2.

To Run a DOS Shell Command

1. From the Ready mode, select **File**, then **Utilities**, and then **DOS Shell**. A dialog box will appear with the prompt *Enter DOS Command, Press Enter for full DOS Shell.*

2. Type the program name that you wish to run, such as C:\WORDSTAR\WS, or the DOS command CHKDSK, and press ↵. To go to the DOS prompt, press ↵ without specifying a program to run.

3. If you have accessed the DOS prompt (and do not simply run another program), you can return to Quattro Pro by typing **EXIT**.

• **EXAMPLE** Suppose you want to save Quattro Pro spreadsheet to a floppy disk in drive A, but you first need to format the floppy disk.

1. From the Ready mode, select **File**, then **Utilities**, and then **DOS Shell**.

2. Type the command **FORMAT A:** and press ↵.

Quattro Pro will relinquish control to the FORMAT command, which will format your disk in the usual fashion. When the command is finished, control will return to Quattro Pro. Without this convenient feature, you would have to save any open spreadsheets, exit from Quattro Pro, run the FORMAT command, load Quattro Pro, and then load all your spreadsheets.

• **CAUTION** Because Quattro Pro remains in memory, you should exercise a little caution when you use the DOS Shell command.

It is very important that the command you specify not be a memory-resident (TSR) program. This type of program is meant to reside in memory while you work on other programs, and it may seriously conflict with Quattro Pro and all your spreadsheets that are still in memory.

When you go to the DOS prompt to perform various DOS-related tasks, it is all too easy to forget that Quattro Pro is still waiting in memory. Don't mistakenly "return" to Quattro Pro by running the program a second time by typing Q. Just type EXIT at the DOS prompt and Quattro Pro will take control once again.

If you will be doing more than just a simple task outside of Quattro Pro, safe practice dictates that you should save any open spreadsheets before invoking the DOS Shell command. This ensures that even if any problems are encountered, your work will already be safely stored on disk.

See Also   File–Exit

FILE MANAGER

When you issue the File–Utilities–File Manager command, a new File Manager window opens. The commands found within the File Manager are covered in Part IV of this book.

SQZ!

The settings under the File–Utilities–SQZ! command let you adjust the parameters for Quattro Pro's file-compression utility, SQZ!. Whenever you save a file, you can choose to have SQZ! compress the file as it is saved to disk. The size of the resulting file will be anywhere from about 40 to 80 percent smaller than the same file uncompressed. A compressed file will automatically be uncompressed when you load it into Quattro Pro.

To Modify the SQZ! File Compression Settings

1. From the Ready mode, select **File** and then **Utilities**, and then **SQZ!**. The SQZ! menu will appear, and you will see the current setting to the right of each menu item.
2. To change one of the options, select that item from the menu.
3. Select the setting you want from the menu that is offered.
4. Choose Quit to return to the Ready mode.

• **OPTIONS**   The following settings affect the way SQZ! compresses Quattro Pro spreadsheets for the current session of Quattro Pro. To modify the settings and then retain them for all future sessions of Quattro Pro, make the changes and then use the Options–Update command.

Remove Blanks By default, this option is set to No, so that any cell that is empty but has been formatted or unprotected will be saved to disk along with the rest of the spreadsheet. If you set this option to Yes, SQZ! will ignore all empty cells during the save process, thereby saving even more space on disk.

Note that when you later retrieve the file, the empty cells that were ignored will no longer be formatted or unprotected. This is a handy means for stripping out any formatted but otherwise blank cells from your spreadsheet.

Storage of Values When you save a spreadsheet, a cell that contains a formula will have both its formula and the formula's result stored on disk. The Storage of Values option on the SQZ! menu is set by default to Exact, so that when a file is compressed, a formula's result will be saved exactly as it is shown in the spreadsheet, to 15 decimal places. You can change this setting to Approximate to save a little space on disk—a formula's result will be stored only to seven decimal places.

To save more room on disk, you can choose Remove, which strips the result from the formula as the cell is saved to disk. When you later load the spreadsheet back into Quattro Pro, the formulas are recalculated and will once again display their results.

Version There are two versions of SQZ! supported by Quattro Pro, SQZ! and SQZ! Plus. By default, the Version option is set to the newer version, SQZ! Plus. If you wish to save your spreadsheets in the older SQZ! file format, change this setting to SQZ!.

• **NOTES** When specifying a file name while saving a spreadsheet with the File–Save or Tools–Xtract command, you can choose to have SQZ! compress the file by including the appropriate file name extension. There are six compressed file formats:

WQ!: Quattro Pro

WKZ: Quattro 1

WK$: Lotus 1-2-3 Release 1A (.WKS file)

WK!: Lotus 1-2-3 Release 2.01 and 2.2 (.WK1 file)

WR$: Symphony Release 1.2

WR!: Symphony Release 2

For example, if you specified the file name MYFILE.WQ!, SQZ! would compress the file in the standard Quattro Pro compressed-file format. This file could not be read by Quattro or Lotus 1-2-3.

See Also   File–Save, File–Save All, File–Save-As, Tools–Xtract

FILE–WORKSPACE

A *workspace* is the current configuration of open spreadsheet files and File Manager windows, including the position and size of each window. With the File–Workspace–Save command, you can save this configuration to a workspace file. You can later use the File–Workspace–Restore command to recreate the session that was stored in the workspace.

To Create a Workspace

1. From the Ready mode, select **File** and then **Workspace**.
2. Choose **Save** from the Workspace menu.
3. Specify a name for the workspace file. Quattro Pro will automatically append the extension .WSP to the file name.

To Load a Workspace

1. From the Ready mode, select **File** and then **Workspace**.
2. Choose **Restore** from the Workspace menu.
3. Specify the name of the workspace file. If you don't specify a file name extension, Quattro Pro assumes the file extension is .WSP. All the files associated with that workspace will be opened.

- **NOTES** A workspace file does not contain the actual spreadsheets, but only a list of file names that belong to the workspace and the size and position of each window that will be opened. So even when you save a workspace, you must be sure to save your spreadsheets.

Any spreadsheets that are already open in Quattro Pro will remain open, and will not be affected by the spreadsheets that the workspace opens.

See Also File–Open, File–Retrieve, File–Save, File–Save All, File–Save As

GRAPH–ANNOTATE

When you issue the Graph–Annotate command, or press / while viewing a graph, Quattro Pro opens its Graph Annotator and automatically displays the current graph, ready for enhancing. The commands found within the Graph Annotator are covered in Part III of this book.

GRAPH–CUSTOMIZE SERIES

You can modify the attributes of a graph's six series via the options on the Graph–Customize Series command. For pie or column graphs, use the options on the menu under the Graph–Customize Series–Pies command.

BAR WIDTH

The more bars that are shown in a bar graph, the narrower each one will be. But no matter what their width, all bars are drawn to a specific proportion, determined by the Bar Width command.

The default value is 60, so all bars take up about 60 percent of the space allotted to them. You can change the percentage from 20, for skinny bars with lots of space between them, to 90, for fat bars with very little space between them.

COLORS

This command enables you to adjust the color of each of the six series in the graph. To change the colors in a pie or column chart, use the Graph–Customize Series–Pies–Colors command.

FILL PATTERNS

This command enables you to adjust the cross-hatching patterns that are used to distinguish the six series in bar, rotated-bar, stacked-bar, and area charts.

To change the fill pattern in a pie or column chart, use the Graph–Customize Series–Pies–Patterns command.

INTERIOR LABELS

Use this command to add interior labels, which identify the data points in one or more series within the graph. You specify a block in the spreadsheet that contains either text or numbers; it should have the same number of cells as the data series that it will identify.

For line and XY graphs, you can choose where to place the label in relation to the data point. For bar and rotated-bar graphs, the labels always appear above or to the right of each bar. On a stacked bar graph, the labels appear above the bars, but represent only the top data series in the bar. Labels do not appear on pie, column, or area graphs.

MARKERS & LINES

The options on the Markers & Lines menu enable you to change the style of the lines and data-point markers that identify each series in line and XY graphs. There are three options on the menu, each of which lets you change any of the six data series in the graph.

Formats By default, a line with markers is used to indicate each series on line and XY graphs. The Formats option allows you to choose to show only lines, only symbols (markers), both, or neither.

Line Styles The Line Styles option offers eight line styles, including styles such as Solid, Dashed, and Heavy Dashed.

Markers The Markers option lets you choose a marker style for the data points in a series. There are ten marker styles, such as Filled Square, Filled Triangle, or Empty Square.

OVERRIDE TYPE

The Override Type command lets you combine bar and line charts in the same graph. It will function only when the current graph type is bar, line, or XY.

For each of the six data series in the graph, there are three choices available:

- **Default**: The current graph type will be used to plot the series.
- **Bar**: The series will be shown as a bar.
- **Line**: The series will be shown as a line.

PIES

The options on the Pies menu enable you to modify the look of both pie and column charts (the Explode option affects only pie charts).

In a pie graph, the first slice of the pie is the one nearest the top of the circle. The other eight slices are numbered clockwise around the pie. In a column graph, the numbering starts from the bottom segment.

Colors This option sets the color for any of nine pie slices or column sections.

Explode This option enables you to pull out any of the first nine slices from the pie graph (this is not relevant for a column graph) in order to call attention to it.

Label Format You can adjust the format of the numbers that identify each piece of a pie or column graph. Choose either:

- %: The default format style. Each pie wedge or column section is labeled with its percentage of the entire graph.
- **Value**: Shows the actual value associated with each wedge.
- $: Shows the value for each wedge, preceded by a dollar sign.
- **None**: Removes the labeling from the graph.

Patterns This option sets the interior pattern for any of the first nine pie slices or column sections.

Tick Marks Tick marks are the lines that connect each wedge of the pie or segment of a column to its label. Choose **Yes** to show the tick marks (the default) or **No** to hide them.

RESET

When you want to start a new graph that is not built on any previous settings, use the Graph–Customize Series–Reset command. It allows you to undefine any or all of the six data series (including their associated interior labels) and the x-axis series. You can also reset all graph settings to their defaults.

Before you reset all the graph settings, be sure that you either do not want to keep the current graph, or that you have preserved it by giving it a name with the Graph–Names–Create command.

UPDATE

Each time you load Quattro Pro, all of its command options are set to their default status. Use Graph–Customize Series–Update if you want to save your current graph settings as system defaults.

Y-AXIS

When you are creating a bar, line, or XY graph and need to compare data series that vary widely in scale, select **Secondary Y-Axis** to plot one or more of the six data series against a second y-axis. You can change a series back with the **Primary Y-Axis** command.

In Figure II.4, a graph plots the monthly water flows of a river and one of its tributaries. The y-axis on the left is for the tributary, and it is scaled from 200 to 500. The secondary y-axis on the right is for the river, and it has a much larger scale, running from 19,000 to 26,000. Each y-axis has been labeled to clearly indicate exactly what is being shown.

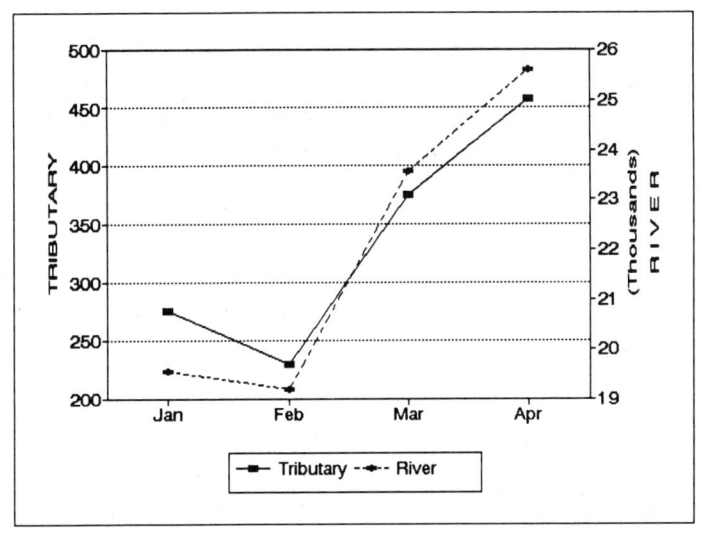

Figure II.4: A second y-axis compares two widely varying data ranges

GRAPH–FAST GRAPH

With the Graph–Fast Graph command, you can create a graph in one step, defining all the graph's data series as well as the x-axis labels and the cells for the legend.

To Create a Graph in One Step

1. From the Ready mode, select **Graph** and then **Fast Graph** (Ctrl-G).

2. Specify the block that contains the graph data, x-axis labels, and legends, and press . The graph will be built from the data in the block and drawn on the screen.

3. To return to the spreadsheet, press any key. You can continue to enhance the graph at this point.

• **NOTES** When you use the Fast Graph command, Quattro Pro makes a few assumptions about the data in the block you specify. If the data has more rows than columns, it assumes the graph series should be arranged by columns. If there are more columns than rows, the series will be arranged by rows.

The x-axis labels are taken from either the column on the left or the row at the top of the block, depending on whether the series are being arranged by columns or rows. The legends will be taken from either the first column or row—wherever the labels are not.

• **CAUTION** Before invoking the Graph–Fast Graph command, you may want to save the current graph by giving it a name with the Graph–Name–Create command. If you then want to draw a completely new graph with the Fast Graph command, you will generally want to use the Graph–Customize Series–Reset–Graph command to clear all the current settings from the graph menu. That way, you will know that you are starting fresh when you define the new graph.

See Also Graph–Name–Create, Graph–Series, Graph–Text–Legends

GRAPH–GRAPH TYPE

Quattro Pro has a variety of graph styles from which to choose, and you use the Graph–Graph Type command to select one for the current graph. The type of graph you choose depends to a great extent on the type of data you are graphing, and how crowded the graph will become once you have enhanced it. For example, if you have many points to graph, a line graph is generally more appropriate than a bar graph.

To Select a New Graph Type

1. From the Ready mode, select **Graph** and then **Graph Type**.
2. Choose a graph type from the list of graphs offered. (A graphical representation of each graph is shown when Quattro Pro is in WYSIWYG mode.)

• **OPTIONS** Once you have defined a graph, you can switch graph types at any time to view your data in a different style.

Area Similar to a stacked-bar graph, the area graph accumulates the total for the series. Use an area graph when you need to plot many data series, as it is less cluttered than a stacked-bar graph.

Bar A bar graph is built from rectangles, the heights of which represent the magnitude of the data. Because the bars are drawn from the lowest end of the y-axis (where it meets the x-axis), the y-axis scale usually starts at zero.

Column This option graphs a single data series, just as a pie graph does, except the values are shown as blocks in a column instead of as slices in a pie.

High-Low The data series are plotted in pairs. Each pair of data points (the low and high) are plotted as a single vertical line, with the line's bottom the low value and its top the high value.

Line The x-axis consists of text labels laid out evenly along the axis. Points for each series are plotted from left to right and connected with a line. Use a line graph when there are many data points to plot.

Pie This option graphs a single data series, just as a column graph does. Each value is represented by a wedge in the pie. The wedges are sized in relation to their values.

Rotated-Bar A rotated bar graph is a bar graph that has been rotated 90 degrees, so that the bars run from left to right. The positions of the two axes are switched, so that the x-axis is the vertical line on the left, and the y-axis is the horizontal line at the bottom of the graph.

Stacked Bar A stacked-bar graph is similar to a bar graph, but instead of a separate bar for each series, the data for each one is stacked on the other to build the bar. The total is represented by the height of the bar, and the contribution of each series to the bar is shown. The accumulation of the series works well with data that contributes to a total. For example, using a stacked bar graph to plot home energy consumption for gas, oil, and electricity would produce bars that show total home energy consumption.

Text Quattro Pro's Graph Annotator has some powerful tools for enhancing graphs, and you may frequently want to create a "graph" that has no graph in it. That's when you specify a text graph. All the usual graph settings are ignored for a text graph, and only the features you add using the Graph Annotator are shown.

XY An XY graph is similar to a line graph, but the x-axis consists of numbers, and the tick marks are sorted and spaced according to their values. This is a particularly important distinction when you are plotting the data series against other numeric data on the x-axis.

3-D Graphs There are four graph types listed under the 3-D Graphs choice: **Bar**, **Ribbon**, **Step**, and **Area**. The primary difference between a three-dimensional graph and other Quattro Pro graph types is that the data series (up to six) are laid out from front to back. All four 3-D graphs can be used to plot the same data. Select a style that best suits the trends or comparisons that you are trying to show.

GRAPH–HIDE

When you have placed a graph in the spreadsheet with the Graph–Insert command, you can remove that graph with the Graph–Hide command.

To Remove a Graph from the Spreadsheet

1. From the Ready mode, select **Graph** and then **Hide**. A dialog box will be displayed showing all the named graphs you have created, as well as one called Current Graph.

2. Choose the graph that you want to remove from the spreadsheet (one that you have previously inserted into the spreadsheet).

See Also   Graph–Insert

GRAPH–INSERT

You can view one graph at a time with the Graph–View command (F10), but you can also insert up to eight graphs into the spreadsheet with the Graph–Insert command. You can then view the graph and your spreadsheet data at the same time, and watch the graph change as you change the data. You can also print your spreadsheet and graph together.

To Insert a Graph into the Spreadsheet

1. From the Ready mode, select **Graph** and then **Insert**. A dialog box will be displayed showing all the named graphs you have created, as well as one called Current Graph.

72 Spreadsheet Operations

   2. Choose the graph that you want to insert into the spreadsheet.

   3. Specify the block where you would like the graph displayed and press ↵.

• **NOTES** In order to see graphs within the spreadsheet, you must use the Options–Display Mode–WYSIWYG command to put the spreadsheet into graphics mode. However, you must have an EGA or VGA video display to do so.

If the spreadsheet is in text mode (the 80 × 25 command on the Options–Display mode menu), an inserted graph will appear as a highlighted box. But the graph will be printed when you print your spreadsheet to the Graphics Printer.

The graph will overlay the display of any data in the cells that it occupies, but the data will still be there, and can be referenced in formulas or copied to other locations. The larger the block that you specify for the graph, the larger the graph will be, but Quattro Pro will by default maintain a 4 to 3 aspect ratio between the graph's width and its height. If you want to size the graph to fit a certain block size, first set the Print–Graph Print–Layout–4:3 Aspect command to No.

When the cursor is on a cell covered by an inserted graph, instead of showing the cell contents, the input line will show the cell address and the name of the graph, such as

Graph C12: *<Current Graph>*

As long as the cursor is on an inserted graph, that graph becomes the current graph. If you press F10, that is the graph you will see displayed.

See Also Graph–Hide, Print–Destination–Graphics Printer, Print–Graph Print–Layout, Options–Display Mode

GRAPH–NAME

Only one graph in the spreadsheet is the current graph. It is the one you see when you invoke the Graph View command or press F10. You can modify that graph in any way to create a different graph, but the first graph will be gone, replaced by the new one. To save a graph for future use, use the commands on the Graph–Name menu: Autosave Edits, Create, Display, Erase, Graph Copy, Reset, and Slide Show.

AUTOSAVE EDITS (Version 3 only)

In Quattro Pro 3, this command helps to avoid the loss of the current graph settings when you use the Graph–Name–Display command before you have saved the current settings with the Graph–Name–Create command.

By default, Autosave Edits is set to No. When you choose Yes, any changes you make to a graph will be saved automatically whenever you call up another graph and replace the current one. For this command to work, the current graph must already be named.

- **CAUTION** If you plan to revise the current graph and save it under a new name, you must either turn off Autosave Edits or name the graph before you make any changes. Otherwise, the command will save your changes under the original name and replace the original graph.

See Also Graph–Name–Create

CREATE

To Create a Name for the Current Graph

1. From the Graph–Name menu, select **Create**. A dialog box will be displayed showing all of the named graphs that you have already created.

2. Choose a graph name from the list to assign the current graph settings to that name, or type in a graph name and press ↵.

- **NOTES** A graph name can have as many as 15 characters. Once you have named the current graph, you can reset the graph settings or modify them to create a new graph. Later, you can recall the named graph (make it the current graph) with the Graph–Name–Display command.

- **CAUTION** When you recall a graph with the Graph–Name–Display command and then revise that graph, be sure to save the graph again with the Graph–Name–Create command; otherwise, you will lose any changes you've made.

See Also Graph–Name–Display, Print–Graph Print–Destination

DISPLAY

To Make a Named Graph the Current One

1. From the Graph–Name menu, select **Display**. A dialog box will be displayed showing all the named graphs you have created.

2. Choose a graph name from the list or type in a graph name and press ↵.

- **NOTES** The graph you select with Graph–Name–Display will immediately be displayed on the screen and become the current graph, replacing the previous current graph. If you modify this graph, you must save it again in order to retain the changes—use the Graph–Name–Create command.

- **CAUTION** If you forget to save the current graph with the Graph–Name–Create command, displaying a named graph with Graph–Name–Display will completely replace all your work. Be sure to save your graph before moving on to another one.

See Also Graph–Name–Autosave Edits

ERASE

To Erase a Graph Name

1. From the Graph–Name menu, select **Erase**. A dialog box will be displayed showing all the named graphs you have created.

2. Choose a graph name from the list, or type in a graph name and press ↵. That name and its associated graph will be removed from the spreadsheet.

GRAPH COPY

To Copy a Graph to Another Spreadsheet

The two spreadsheets, the source and target, must both be in memory, and the source spreadsheet must be the active one.

1. From the Graph–Name menu, select **Graph Copy**. A dialog box will be displayed showing all the named graphs you have created.

2. Choose a graph name from the list or type in a graph name and press ↵.

3. Point to any cell in the target spreadsheet using any of the usual Quattro Pro methods for moving between windows: Click the mouse in the target window, select the window from the list when you press Alt-0, or press Alt and the window's number. Or, type in the name of the spreadsheet using linking formula syntax, such as [C:\DATA\MYFILE]A1.

- **NOTES** The graph that is created in the target spreadsheet will still refer to the data in the source spreadsheet. If you want to use this graph with data in its own spreadsheet, you must select new cells for each data series.

RESET

To Reset All Graph Names

1. From the Graph–Name menu, select **Reset**.
2. A menu with the choices No and Yes will appear. Choose **No** to cancel the command or choose **Yes** to erase all graph names and their associated graphs from the spreadsheet.

SLIDE

To Create a Graphics Slide Show

1. From the Ready mode, select **Graph**, then **Name**, and then **Slide**.
2. Specify the block that contains the graph names and display times, and in Quattro Pro 3, the optional columns for transition effects and speed, and sound files. The first graph named in the first column will be displayed as the slide show begins.

- **OPTIONS** The slide show definition block consists of up to two columns in Quattro Pro 2 and up to five columns in Quattro Pro 3, and one row for each slide. Enter the following information in each column, from left to right:

  - Name of Graph: The name of the graphs to display.

  - Display Duration: The time, in seconds, that each graph should be displayed. Leaving the cell blank, or entering a 0, means that the graph will be displayed until you press any key (or click the left mouse button) to continue with the next graph.

  - Transition Effect (Quattro Pro 3 only): The number, from 1 to 24, of the graph transition effect. If you specify no effect by entering a zero or leaving the cell blank, the default effect is used, which is simply one graphics screen instantly replacing the previous one. The other effects are variations on five different styles, including the fade (2), sideways and vertical wipes (3–10), spiral (11–17), and dissolves

(18–24). A list of effects is shown on the Quattro Pro help screens for the Slide command.

- Transition Speed (Quattro Pro 3 only): The speed at which the transition to the next graph happens, with a 0 or a blank cell being the fastest. The slower speeds are often too slow to be practical.

- Sound File (Quattro Pro 3 only): The name of a digitized sound file that will be played during the transition. Several sound files come with Quattro Pro; each has a file name extension of .SND. You can also play a sound file via a graph button and with the macro command {play}.

While viewing the slide show, press the Backspace key or the right mouse button to view the previous graph in the slide.

See Also   Part III: Graph Annotator—Pick–Bkg Button, Text–Graph Button

GRAPH–OVERALL

The options on the Graph–Overall menu let you change the appearance of the entire graph.

To Modify the Overall Look of the Graph

1. From the Ready mode, select **Graph** and then **Overall**.
2. Select one of the options from the Overall menu to change that aspect of the graph.

● **OPTIONS**   You can experiment with each of these options to achieve the right look for your graph.

Background Color   Use this command to change the color of the background outside of the graph. Choose a color from the menu that is offered. Use the Graph–Overall–Grid–Fill Color command to change the background color within the graph.

78 Spreadsheet Operations

Color/B&W To remove all the colors from a graph and make it black and white, choose **B&W** from the Graph–Overall–Color/B&W command. Or, choose **Color** to return the graph to color, the default.

Drop Shadow Color (Version 3 only) This command lets you specify the color of the shadow that will be used for text to which you have assigned a drop shadow. You first choose the color of the text that you want to affect, and then select the color for its drop shadow.

Grid By default, Quattro Pro draws horizontal grid lines across the graph from each labeled tick mark on the y-axis. These lines help you pinpoint the value of the bars or data points on the graph. You can change the grid with the Graph–Overall–Grid command. Choose:

Horizontal: Draws grid lines across the graph (the default).

Vertical: Draws grid lines from the x-axis.

Both: Draws both horizontal and vertical grid lines.

Clear: Removes all grid lines from the graph.

You can also change the look of the grid from this menu:

Grid Color: Changes the color of the grid lines; choose from the colors that are offered.

Line Style: Choose the line style for the grid lines (the default is dotted lines).

Fill Color: Specifies the color behind the grid lines, within the body of the graph; choose from the colors that are offered.

Outlines You can choose to have boxes drawn around the graph's main titles, its legends, and the graph itself. By default, the graph's legends are enclosed in a box, but the titles and graph itself are not.

The commands on the Outlines menu are **Titles**, **Legends**, and **Graph**. Each brings up the same menu of box types, including **Box**, **Shadow**, and **Sculpted** (in Quattro Pro 3 only).

Three-D By default, the components of pie, bar, and column charts are all drawn with a third dimension. You can set the Three-D option to **No** to draw these graphs as two-dimensional.

GRAPH–SERIES

With the options under the Graph–Series command, you define the data that is to be graphed. You can specify from one to six series of data for all graphs except pie or column charts, which plot only one series. In the graph, each series appears as a different color or style of bar, line, or marker. You can use the Graph–Customize Series command to change any of these attributes for each series.

You can also specify the x-axis labels (the block of text or value cells that appears along the x-axis in the graph) while you are defining the data series. You can modify the x-axis settings by using options on the Graph–X-Axis menu.

When the data series you are graphing all reside in a single block, you can use the Graph–Series–Group command to specify all of them in one step.

To Specify the Data Series or X-Axis Labels

1. From the Ready mode, select **Graph** and then **Series**.

2. Select one of the six series, **1st Series** through **6th Series**, or select **X-Axis Series**.

3. Specify the block that contains the data for the selected series and press ↵.

4. Repeat step 2 for another series, or choose **Quit** to return to the Graph menu.

● **NOTES** A block for a series can be in the current spreadsheet or in another spreadsheet in memory or on disk.

When you graph more than one series, the cells of each series do not have to be adjacent. However, each series should have the same number of cells. That way, corresponding points in each series will be tied to the same tick mark on the x-axis.

The entries in the block you define as the X-Axis Labels will appear along the x-axis of the graph. In all but the XY graph, these will be evenly distributed along the x-axis. In XY graphs, they will be spaced and sorted according to their numeric value.

To Specify the Data Series as One Group

1. From the Ready mode, select **Graph**, then **Series**, and then **Group**.
2. Specify the block that contains all the columns or rows of data that you wish to graph, and press . You will be offered a menu with the choices Columns and Rows.
3. Choose **Columns** if the data is arranged by columns or **Rows** if the data is arranged by rows.

Each column or row of data will be assigned to one of the six data series.

See Also   Graph–Fast Graph

GRAPH–TEXT

By using the options on the Graph–Text menu, you can add text to several key parts of your graph: a two-line title at the top, titles for the x- and y-axes, and legends for the data series. You can also select the font and style for the text.

To Enter Text into the Graph

1. From the Ready mode, select **Graph** and then **Text**.

2. From the menu that is offered, select the element of the graph for which you want to enter text: **1st Line, 2nd Line, X-Title, Y-Title, or Secondary Y-Title**. Or, choose **Legends**, and then choose one of the six graph series for which you want to create a legend. You can also choose Position from this menu and specify the position of the legends in the graph: **Bottom**, **Right**, or **None**.

3. Type in the text and press . Or type a backslash (\) and the cell address or block name of the cell that contains the title.

- **OPTIONS** You can enter as many as 39 characters of text into each text element of the graph (only 19 characters are allowed for the legend for each data series). Figure II.5 illustrates where these titles appear in the graph.

1st Line: The main title, positioned by default at the top of the graph

2nd Line: The secondary title, located below the 1st Line title

X-Title: The title beneath the x-axis

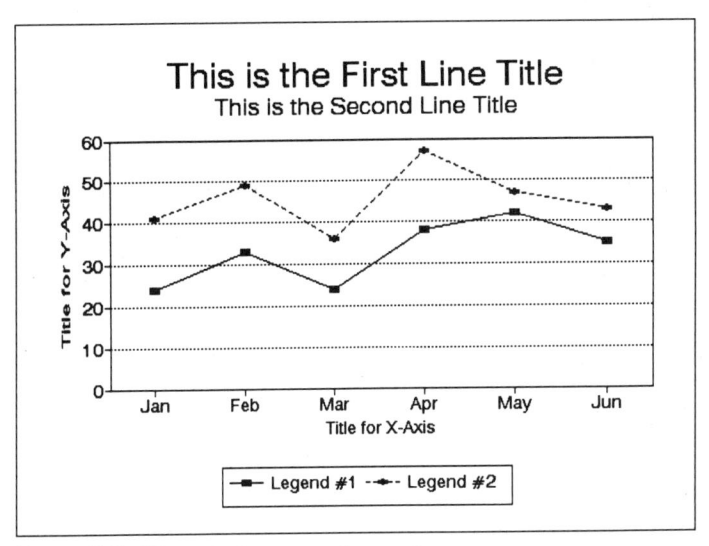

Figure II.5: The text elements of a graph

Y-Title: The title to the left of the y-axis

Secondary Y-Axis: The title to the right of the secondary y-axis

Legends: The text that identifies each of the 6 graph series

You can adjust the font and style for any of these with the Graph–Text–Font command.

• **NOTES**   You can also enter text into a graph with the Graph Annotator. You can't use it to create the key text elements of a graph, such as the first and second titles, but you can use the Graph Annotator to edit and position any of the text elements.

Referencing a Cell: Instead of entering text, you can enter a backslash and a cell address to reference the text in that cell. For example, entering \B19 would display in the graph title the text from cell B19. As many characters as will fit will be shown in the graph. Unlike a formula, a cell reference does not adjust to changes in the spreadsheet. To use this method safely, either make sure that the text cell never moves or refer to a block name instead.

Entering Bullets: You can include a bullet character in the graph's titles and legends by using the special bullet code, **bullet** *n*\, where *n* is a number from 0 to 6. The bullet will be displayed when you view or print the graph. Note that the bullet code uses 10 characters out of the 39-character maximum.

To Change the Font for Text in the Graph

1. From the Ready mode, select **Graph**, then **Text**, and then **Font**.
2. From the menu that is offered, select the element of the graph for which you want to modify text. You are offered a menu of font attributes.
3. Select any of the four font attribute options on the menu.

• **OPTIONS**   The graph text locations available on the Font menu include those found on the Graph–Text menu: 1st Line, 2nd

Line, X-Title, Y-Title, and Legends. It also includes Data & Tick Labels, which lets you change the font for the x-axis labels.

Four options appear when you select any of the graph text elements:

Typeface: The character set, such as Roman, Sans Serif, Bitstream Courier, and Bitstream Dutch

Point Size: The size of the characters, measured in points

Style: Bold, italic, underlined, drop shadow (in Quattro Pro 3 only), or reset (no style)

Color: The color in which the font will be displayed on a color monitor or printed on a color printer

The Drop Shadow option (in Quattro Pro 3 only) under the Style command is not found on the Style–Fonts–Edit Fonts menu. Use it to have the text drawn with a contrasting drop shadow.

You can also change any of these text attributes from within the Graph Annotator.

See Also   Style–Font, Part III: Graph Annotator–Text

GRAPH-VIEW

The Graph–View command (F10) displays the current graph on the screen. While you are working in the graph menus, you can press F10 at any time to view your graph; you don't have to go back to the main Graph menu and invoke the View command.

To View the Current Graph

1. From the Ready mode, select **Graph** and then **View**, or press F10 from the Ready or Menu mode.
2. The current graph will be displayed on the screen.
3. To return to the spreadsheet or menu, press any key.

GRAPH–X-AXIS AND GRAPH–Y-AXIS

You can tailor the look of your graph's x- and y-axes with the options on the Graph–X-Axis and Graph–Y-Axis commands. Both menus are almost identical; each has one command that is not on the other.

To Adjust the Look of the Graph's Axes

1. From the Ready mode, select **Graph** and then **X-Axis** or **Y-Axis**.

2. Select one of the axes options from the menu and adjust it accordingly.

3. Repeat step 2 for another option or choose **Quit** to return to the Graph menu.

• **OPTIONS**   Figure II.6 illustrates all the options on the X-Axis and Y-Axis menus. The first three options on each of those menus affect the scale of the respective axis:

Scale: Quattro Pro automatically scales the minimum and maximum values on the axes to contain the smallest and largest data points in the graph. To set the axis limits manually, set the Scale command to Manual and enter Low and High values. For the x-axis, the Scale command is relevant only in an XY graph.

Low: Specify the smallest value for the axis. A graph that has only positive values is often more readable when you set this option to 0.

High: Specify the highest value for the axis. When the points on one data series soar far higher than any of the other series, it is sometimes helpful to lower the maximum value of the y-axis in order to "zoom in" on the more populated portion of the graph.

Graph–X-Axis and Graph–Y-Axis

The next four options on the Graph–X-Axis and Graph–Y-Axis menus affect the tick marks along the respective axes:

Alternate Ticks: Alleviates crowding of the text along the x-axis by creating two rows of text, as shown in Figure II.6 (this option is not available on the Y-Axis menu).

Display Scaling: When the numbers on the axes are too large to display without crowding, Quattro Pro automatically scales them by factors of ten. If you want the complete numbers to show (and no scaling to take place), set the Display Scaling command to No.

Format of Ticks: Gives the numbers along the axes a numeric format, just as you use the Style–Numeric format command to format a cell in the spreadsheet. In Figure II.6, the y-axis values have been given a Currency format with zero decimals.

Increment: Enter the number that will be used to increment the tick marks along the axis. In Figure II.6, the increment is 25 for the y-axis.

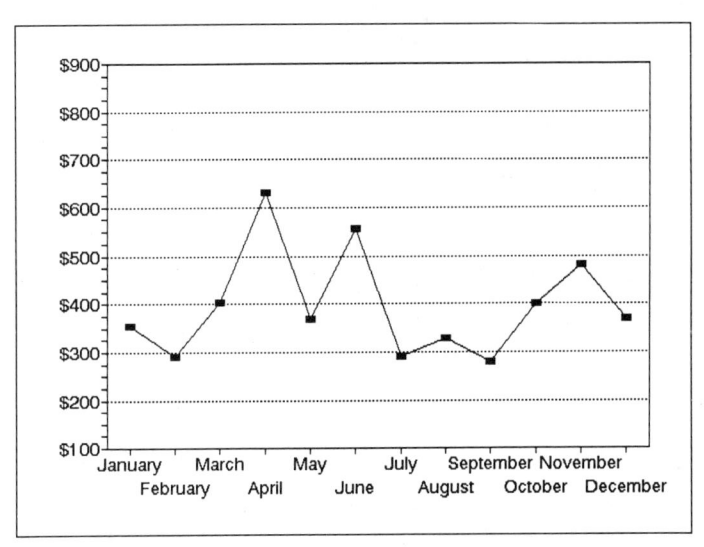

Figure II.6: Sample graph with the X-axis and Y-axis options

Mode: When the data in the graph scales a very wide range along the y-axis, such as thousands to billions, you can choose Log from the Mode menu to scale all the data logarithmically. Be sure to label one of the graph titles to indicate this change of scale.

No. of Minor Ticks: Set the number of unlabeled tick marks that will appear along the axis. The default is 0, so Quattro Pro labels every tick. In Figure II.9, this option is set to 3.

2nd Y-Axis: When you have turned on a graph's second y-axis via the Graph–Customize Series–Y-Axis command, you can modify the look of that axis with the Graph–Y-Axis–2nd Y-Axis command. It has the same options as the Graph–Y-Axis menu.

See Also   Graph–Customize Series, Graph–Series

OPTIONS–COLORS

Use this command to change the colors of many of the Quattro Pro screen components, such as the menu, desktop, spreadsheet, and help screens. If you have a monochrome video display, your choices will be limited to normal, bold, underline, inverse, and empty.

To Adjust the Colors of Quattro Pro

1. From the Ready mode, select **Options** and then **Colors**. A menu will appear listing various portions of the Quattro Pro program, such as Menu and Spreadsheet.

2. Highlight the item whose colors you wish to change and press ↵ or click with your mouse.

3. Choose a color from the color palette. The current color for the selected item is indicated by a small rotating line.

Either move the rotating line to a new color and press ↵, or click on a color with your mouse.

4. Choose another area of the program for which you want to modify the colors, or choose Quit to return to Ready mode.

● **OPTIONS** To make the color changes permanent, use the Options–Update command.

In Quattro Pro 3, to change the spreadsheet colors when you are running in graphics mode (Options–Display Mode–WYSIWYG), use the Options–Colors–Spreadsheet–WYSIWYG Colors command.

The choices on the Colors–Conditional menu let you specify a color for specific numeric values in the spreadsheet.

On/Off: By default, all the options on the conditional menu are turned off. Set this to **Enable** in order to have them take effect.

Greatest Normal Value: The highest value in the acceptable range.

Smallest Normal Value: The lowest value in the acceptable range.

Below Normal Color: The color for cells whose contents fall below the smallest normal value.

Normal Cell Color: The color for cells whose contents fall between the smallest and greatest normal values inclusive.

Above Normal Color: The color for cells whose contents fall above the greatest normal value.

ERR: Color for cells with results equivalent to @ERR. By default, these are red on black.

OPTIONS–DISPLAY MODE

Depending on the capabilities of your video adapter and display monitor, you can change the output of your display with the Options–Display Mode command.

- **OPTIONS** The menu offered by the Display Mode command will vary, depending on the type of video adapter in your computer. On a VGA system, there will be many brand-specific choices that give the best settings for those video adapters. There are also four basic choices that should be available on all VGA systems:

A: 80x25: The standard text display on DOS computers; provides 80 characters across the screen and 25 lines.

B: WYSIWYG (Version 3); Graphics mode (Versions 2 and SE): Graphics mode, where fonts and inserted graphs are displayed in the spreadsheet as they will appear when printed.

C: EGA: 80x43: Enhanced text mode, 43 lines on the screen.

D: VGA: 80x50: Enhanced text mode, 50 lines on the screen.

The WYSIWYG graphics-mode display offers you the benefits of on-screen fonts, inserted graphs, row heights, and cell enhancements, but you pay the penalty of a much slower screen-refresh rate. Note that in Quattro Pro versions 2 and SE, the equivalent command was Graphics Mode, and that fonts were not shown as they would be printed.

When you are using the WYSIWYG mode, the quality of the on-screen fonts is determined by the Options–Graphics Quality command.

If you make changes that you wish to keep for future sessions in Quattro Pro, use the Options–Update command.

See Also Options–Graphics Quality

OPTIONS–FORMATS

Use the choices on the Options–Formats menu to change the global default settings for numeric formats, label alignment, column widths, and the display of zeros for the current spreadsheet.

- **OPTIONS** The global settings on the Options–Format menu (Align Labels, Global Width, and Numeric Format) serve as the defaults for all cells in the current spreadsheet. You can override these defaults for a block of cells by using the equivalent commands on the Style menu: Alignment, Column Width and Block Size–Set Width, and Numeric Format, respectively.

Align Labels   This command sets the label alignment of all text cells in the current spreadsheet. It offers the choices **Left**, **Right**, and **Center**. To change the alignment of numeric cells, use the Style–Alignment command.

Global Width   Use this command to change the width of all columns in the current spreadsheet.

Hide Zeros   Choose **Yes** to hide the display of all zeros in the current spreadsheet. You can display the zeros by choosing **No**, the default.

Numeric Format   This command sets the numeric format of all cells in the current spreadsheet. It offers all the same format styles that are found on the Style–Numeric Format menu.

OPTIONS–GRAPHICS QUALITY

There are two levels of graphics quality in Quattro Pro that affect the printing of fonts and their display on the screen when the spreadsheet is in WYSIWYG mode: draft and final.

• **OPTIONS**   The highest quality fonts in Quattro Pro are the Bitstream fonts, which come in Dutch, Swiss, and Courier styles (you can purchase other styles, as well). In order to use them, however, Quattro Pro must build a file on disk for each specific size and style, such as Bitstream Dutch 12-point bold.

Quattro Pro builds a font file when it is needed. You will see the message

Now building fonts

and there will be a delay as the font is built.

You will want to avoid building too many fonts, however, because each one takes up disk space and also takes time to produce (perhaps a minute for a large font on a slow computer).

When the spreadsheet is in the 80×25 display mode, the Options–Graphics Quality command has no effect on the spreadsheet display. But it does affect the display of fonts in the Graph Annotator and Screen Preview. It also affects the quality of your printouts and how long they take to produce when you have set the Print–Destination command to Graphics Printer.

Draft   This is the mode you will want to use for most work; select Final only when you need a high-quality display or printout. In Draft mode, when you have chosen a Bitstream font for a block with the Style–Font command, Quattro Pro will display or print the font only if its font file already exists on disk. It will not take the time to build it, but will instead substitute one of the Hershey fonts, which are of lesser quality but do not require separate font files.

Final   When you have chosen Final and have set Options–Display Mode to WYSIWYG, Quattro Pro will display or print all fonts you have selected, even if it must first build the necessary font files. You will have the best possible display or printout, but you may have to tolerate the delay as Quattro Pro builds them.

In order to have the highest quality printouts, set the Print–Destination command to Graphics Printer, and the Options–Display Mode command to Final.

See Also   Print–Destination–Graphics Printer, Style–Font

OPTIONS–HARDWARE

There are some devices, such as your printer, that Quattro Pro cannot detect. The choices on the Options–Hardware menu let you specify your computer's video display and printer, and shows you the current status of your computer's memory and math coprocessor.

MEMORY STATUS

On the Hardware menu are three displays that tell you how much memory is available in your computer and whether or not it has a math coprocessor (versions before Quattro Pro 3 provide less memory information).

Normal Memory   This refers to the standard memory that DOS computers have. It shows the amount of memory currently available, the total amount available for spreadsheets, and the percent of the total that is still available.

EMS Memory   If your computer is set up with expanded (EMS) memory, this setting shows the amount of expanded memory currently available, the total amount available for spreadsheets, and the percent of the total that is still available.

Coprocessor   This setting should show Yes if your computer has a math coprocessor installed or an Intel 80486 processor, which has a built-in coprocessor. Quattro Pro can perform certain mathematical calculations many times faster when there is a coprocessor present.

See Also   Options–Other–Expanded Memory

MOUSE BUTTON (VERSION 3 ONLY)

Quattro Pro 3 uses only a single button on your mouse. By default, that button is the one on the left. If you use the mouse in your left hand, you may find it more convenient to make the right mouse button the active one.

To Switch Mouse Buttons

1. From the Ready mode, select **Options**, then **Hardware**, and then **Mouse Button**.
2. Choose **Right** to make the right mouse button the active one.
3. If you want to keep this change for future sessions in Quattro Pro, use the Options–Update command.

PRINTERS

When you installed Quattro Pro, you answered questions about your computer's printer and, optionally, a second printer. That information was used to set the options on the Printers menu. If you change printers, need to refine your selections, or want to change the default printer, adjust the options on this menu accordingly.

To Select a New Printer

1. From the Options–Hardware menu, select **Printers** and then **1st Printer** or **2nd Printer**. A menu of printer options appears.
2. Select the settings for the printer you wish to install.
3. If you wish to keep these changes for future sessions in Quattro Pro, use the Options–Update command.

- **OPTIONS** The Printers menu shows you the make, model, and mode of the currently defined printer, and offers the following choices for modifying the current printer settings or defining a new printer.

Type of Printer Choose the brand name of the printer from the menu that is offered, such as Epson. Then choose the model name, such as EX-1000. Finally, choose a graphics resolution mode for the printer, such as B&W 120 × 216 (8.5 × 11).

Device Choose the port to which the printer is connected, such as Parallel-1 or Serial-1.

Baud Rate, Parity, and Stop Bits If your printer is connected to a serial port, you can specify these serial communications parameters. Usually, you will not need to adjust these, but if you are having printing problems, refer to your printer manual and then adjust them accordingly.

To Select the Default Printer

1. From the Options–Hardware menu, select **Default Printer**.
2. Choose **1st Printer** (normally, the default printer) to make that printer the default. Or, choose **2nd Printer** to make that printer the default.

To Adjust Your Printer's Font Settings

1. From the Options–Hardware menu, select **Printers** and then **Fonts**.
2. Choose either LaserJet Fonts or Autoscale Fonts.

• **OPTIONS** The options on the Fonts menu let you specify your LaserJet font cartridges and gray-shading darkness. You can also choose how fonts are scaled in your graphs.

LaserJet Fonts If you are using a LaserJet or compatible printer, choose either **Left Cartridge** or **Right Cartridge** to specify which cartridge you will be defining. Then select the cartridge from the list that is offered. You will be returned to the Printers menu.

The LaserJet Fonts–Shading Level command in Quattro Pro 3 lets you adjust the darkness of gray shading in LaserJet printouts, such as shading applied with the Style–Shading command. Increase the number in the setting to darken gray shading, or decrease it to lighten shaded areas.

Autoscale Fonts This determines how Quattro Pro treats fonts in your graphs when you change the size of the graph. Normally, Autoscale Fonts is set to **Yes**, so that Quattro Pro automatically scales the fonts to match the graph size. If you shrink the size of the graph, the size of any text in it will also shrink.

If you want to retain the precise font size that you choose for graph text, set this option to **No**.

To Set Other Printer Options

1. From the Options–Hardware menu, select **Printers**.
2. Choose one of the options: **Auto LF**, **Plotter Speed**, or **Single Sheet**.

- **OPTIONS** The following printer options are available.

Auto LF This option instructs the printer to execute a line feed at the end of each printed line. By default this is set to **No** because most printers do this automatically. If you are having problems printing, refer to your printer manual before changing Auto LF to **Yes**.

Plotter Speed This command specifies the speed at which Quattro Pro will print to a plotter. By default this is set to **0**, meaning that no adjustments will be made, and the plotter will run at its preset speed. Change this setting from **1** (slow) to **9** (fast) to allow for printing to different types of media or with different types of pens.

Single Sheet If your printer does not use continuous-feed paper, change this setting to **Yes**. When printing, Quattro Pro will prompt you to insert a new sheet of paper after every form feed.

SCREEN

This command offers several selections for adjusting the Quattro Pro display. You may never have to access this menu, because Quattro Pro can detect the type of display adapter being used on a standard computer. But there are computer systems on which it will be necessary to make manual adjustments. For example, your portable computer may be using a standard video adapter, such as CGA or EGA, but with a nonstandard display. Quattro Pro will detect the adapter, but not the display itself.

- **OPTIONS** Use the following options to fine-tune Quattro Pro's handling of your computer's video display.

Screen Type This offers a menu of the video drivers available in Quattro Pro. The first item on the list is **Autodetect Driver**, which is the one you will use unless you are having a problem with Quattro Pro and your monitor.

Resolution Some video cards offer more than one resolution setting, and you can select one with this command. You will usually not need to adjust this setting because Quattro Pro picks the best resolution for the job.

Aspect Ratio This lets you adjust the screen aspect ratio (the scale of its width to its height) that Quattro Pro uses when it works in WYSIWYG (graphics) mode. You may need this command if you have a portable computer, for example, that has a screen that is proportionally wider than normal.

Invoke the Aspect Ratio command, and the screen will be put into graphics mode with a circle in the center. If Quattro Pro is working well with your video system, the circle will be round. If it is not round, use the ↑ or ↓ key to adjust the circle's aspect ratio. When it looks round, press ↵ to return to the spreadsheet. Then use the Options–Update command to save this change as the system default.

CGA Snow Suppression By default, this is set to Off. Try changing this to On if you have a CGA video adapter and the screen flickers noticeably when you scroll through the spreadsheet.

OPTIONS–INTERNATIONAL

This command lets you adjust several system-wide options for Quattro Pro. As always, to retain any changes you make for future sessions in Quattro Pro, use the Options–Update command.

- **OPTIONS** The following options appear on the Options–International menu.

Currency This option changes the character that is displayed for a cell that you have formatted as Currency with the Style–Numeric

Format command. Specify one or more characters (the $ is the default) and whether the characters should precede or follow the number in the display.

Date and Time   These two choices determine the style that will be used for the numeric formats called *Long intl.* and *Short intl.,* each of which appears on the Date and Date–Time options on the Style–Numeric Format menu.

LICS Conversion   This option lets you specify how Quattro Pro should handle characters from the Lotus International Character Set (LICS) when you retrieve a 1-2-3 spreadsheet.

By default, LICS Conversion is set to No, so that any incoming LICS characters are translated into their equivalent ASCII characters. If you choose **Yes**, LICS characters are displayed as they appear in Lotus 1-2-3.

Negative (Version 3 only)   In Quattro Pro 3, this option lets you choose between having negative numbers displayed within parentheses (the default) or preceded by a minus sign when a number is formatted with either the Currency or Comma formats on the Style–Numeric Format menu.

Overstrike Print   Some printers (especially older ones) can print only standard alphanumeric characters and cannot print such things as accented characters. Set this option to **Yes**, and Quattro Pro will print many of the otherwise unprintable characters.

Punctuation   This command offers a list of eight choices, which let you specify the character used as the decimal point (a period by default), the separator between thousands in a numeric display, and the separator between arguments in @ functions and macro commands.

Keep in mind that the only time the separator between thousands appears in the display is when you have formatted a cell with either the Currency or Comma formats.

Use Sort Table   This option lets you change the order in which the Database–Sort command sorts your data.

The file ASCII.SOR is the default sort table, and sorts text entries according to their ASCII order. The file INTL.SOR causes data to be sorted in dictionary order where, for example, uppercase A and lowercase A are sorted next to one another.

You can also choose NORDAN.SOR (Norwegian and Danish) or SWEDFIN.SOR (Swedish and Finnish). Each is similar to INTL.SOR, but provides an order that is appropriate for those characters unique to the language.

See Also Database–Sort–Sort Rules, Style–Numeric Format

OPTIONS–MOUSE PALETTE

If you have a mouse and its software (driver) installed, Quattro Pro displays a nine-button mouse palette along the right side of the screen. This command lets you program any of the lower seven buttons on the palette.

To Program a Mouse Palette Button

Here are the steps for programming a button so that it applies a numeric format of Currency with zero decimals to the currently selected cells.

1. From the Ready mode, select **Options** and then **Mouse Palette**.
2. Choose the button you wish to change from the list of seven that is offered.
3. Choose **Text** from the menu that is offered.
4. Press **Escape** to clear the existing text. You are allowed to enter up to three characters, which will be used as the text on the mouse button in the palette.
5. Press the Spacebar, type $, and then press ↵.

6. Choose **Macro** from the menu.

7. Press **Escape** to clear the existing macro. You can enter up to 25 characters that will be executed as a macro when this button is clicked.

8. Enter the macro {/ **Block;Format**}c0~~ and press ↵.

9. Choose **Quit** three times to return to Ready mode.

The mouse button should now display **$**. To test this new button:

10. Move the cursor to a cell that has a numeric entry.

11. With your mouse, click on the $ button on the mouse palette. The cell will be formatted in the Currency format with zero decimals. If you wish to keep the changes to the mouse palette for future sessions in Quattro Pro, use the Options–Update command.

OPTIONS–OTHER

This command offers several options for adjusting the system settings in Quattro Pro. As always, if you make changes that you wish to keep for future sessions in Quattro Pro, use the Options–Update command.

- **OPTIONS** If you make changes to any of these options and wish to retain those changes for future sessions in Quattro Pro, remember to use the Options–Update command.

Clock Display The current spreadsheet's file name is shown in the status line at the bottom of the screen. You can also choose to display the current date and time in the status line. Use the **Standard** or **International** options, or choose **None** to turn off their display (the default).

Expanded Memory If your computer has expanded (EMS) memory, Quattro Pro will use it for storing all or part of each open spreadsheet.

Options–Other

Spreadsheet Data: The default setting. Quattro Pro stores only spreadsheet data in EMS memory; the formatting components remain in conventional memory.

Both: Choose this if you are working on many spreadsheets at the same time, or one or more very large spreadsheets. Both the spreadsheet data and formatting information will be stored in EMS memory.

Format: Choose Format to store just the spreadsheet formatting, but not its data, in EMS memory.

None: Choose None to store everything in normal RAM to produce a minor increase in Quattro Pro's speed.

Once you have changed the Expanded Memory setting, in order for the change to take effect, you must close all open spreadsheets and then load them again.

Macro A macro that must write to the screen runs much more slowly than one that runs while the screen remains unchanged. The Macro options let you choose which areas of the screen should not be rewritten during macro execution.

Both: The default setting. Quattro Pro freezes the entire screen while a macro is executing.

Panel: Freezes the spreadsheet panel (menu and input areas), but allows redraw of the spreadsheet proper (see the {paneloff}–{panelon} macro in Part VI).

Window: Freezes the spreadsheet portion of the screen, but allows redraw of the menus and input area (see the {windowsoff}–{windowson} macro in Part VI).

None: The entire screen is rewritten whenever a macro command induces any activity on it, such as selecting a menu or moving the cell selector.

Paradox If you are working on a network or using Paradox with Quattro Pro via the Paradox Access, you must provide the following information to Quattro Pro:

Network Type: Specify the brand of network you are using; this is set to **Disabled**, by default. If you will be using the Paradox Access on a stand-alone system, set this to **Other**.

Directory: Specify the drive and directory where the PARADOX.NET file is located.

Retries: Enter the number of seconds that Quattro Pro should wait before it again tries to access a previously locked database file. The default is 300 seconds.

Undo   The Edit–Undo command (Alt-F5) cancels your last operation and returns the spreadsheet to its state before that operation. Before you can use this feature, you must first turn it on with the Options–Other–Undo–Enable command. To have Undo enabled always, you can then use the Options–Update command.

OPTIONS–PROTECTION

By default, all cells in the spreadsheet are protected, so that no entries or changes are allowed. But this protection feature does not apply unless you use the Options–Protection–Enable command to turn it on.

When enabled, you will not be able to edit or create entries for any protected cells. You can unprotect a block of cells to allow entries with the Style–Protection–Unprotect command.

See Also   Database–Restrict Input, Style–Protection

OPTIONS–RECALCULATION

The options on the Recalculation menu let you adjust the way Quattro Pro performs its spreadsheet recalculations.

- **OPTIONS**   There are three commands and the circular cell display on the Recalculation menu.

Options–Recalculation

Circular Reference   This indicator on the Recalculation menu shows you the cell address of any circular references. A circular reference occurs when a formula refers to its own cell, either directly or indirectly.

Generally, you will want to avoid all circular references, although there will be times when you will build such a reference into a spreadsheet model. You will know there is a circular condition in the spreadsheet when you see the Circ indicator on the status line. Invoke the Options–Recalculation command, and you will see the address of the circular reference.

Iteration   Normally, recalculation evaluates each formula just once. You can set Iteration to a number higher than one if you want multiple recalculations. You may need this feature when you have built a spreadsheet model that purposely contains circular references.

Mode   There are three different modes of recalculation:

> **Automatic**: This is the same as Background recalculation, but you must wait while Quattro Pro performs the recalculation.
>
> **Background**: By default, Quattro Pro recalculates the spreadsheet every time you make an entry. But it does so in the *background*, so that you can continue to work in the spreadsheet without having to wait for the recalculation to be completed.
>
> **Manual**: Recalculation is turned off, and you must press F9, the Calc key, to recalculate the spreadsheet. When you have made changes to the spreadsheet since the last press of the F9 key, you will see the Calc indicator appear on the status line as a reminder that the spreadsheet calculation has not been updated.

Order   Quattro Pro recalculates the spreadsheet according to the following options:

> **Natural**: This is the default; cells are recalculated in order of dependency. If a formula in cell A5 refers to B10, which contains a formula that refers to yet another cell, cell B10 will be recalculated before A5.

Column-wise: The spreadsheet is recalculated column by column. Formulas in column A are recalculated before formulas in other columns.

Row-wise: The spreadsheet is recalculated row by row. Formulas in row 1 are recalculated before formulas in other rows.

OPTIONS–STARTUP

There are several startup configuration settings that you can adjust and save as the defaults. If you make changes that you wish to keep for future sessions in Quattro Pro, use the Options–Update command.

- **OPTIONS** These options affect the startup configuration of Quattro Pro.

Autoload File Enter a file name for this option. By default, the autoload file name is QUATTRO.WQ1. Each time you load Quattro Pro, it looks in the default directory (see the Directory option) for a spreadsheet with this special autoload name. If it finds it there, it immediately loads that spreadsheet.

Beep By default, Quattro Pro beeps, buzzes, or chirps for various operations, such as error conditions. You can turn off the sound by setting this option to **No**.

Directory Each time you load Quattro Pro, it uses the directory named in this option as the default location for your spreadsheet files. Once Quattro Pro is loaded, you can change the directory for the current session with the File–Directory command.

Edit Menus This command brings up the Menu Builder, with which you can modify Quattro Pro's menus. You can replace the default menu structure with one from disk with the Options–Startup–Menu Tree command.

Revising the menus is not something you should do casually. If you have an important need to do so, refer to Appendix A in the Quattro Pro @ *Functions and Macros* reference manual.

File Extension   If you don't specify a file extension when you are saving a spreadsheet, Quattro Pro will append the extension found under the File Extension option. By default, the extension is .WQ1. You might change the extension if you are creating many spreadsheets that you plan to export to another program; you might use .WK1 for Lotus 1-2-3 files.

Menu Tree   When you load Quattro Pro, it configures its menus by loading the menu file QUATTRO.MU. The program comes with two other menu files that emulate two popular spreadsheets. The file 123.MU contains the Lotus 1-2-3 menu tree, and Q1.MU contains the menu tree for the original Quattro, version 1.

If you want to use one of these other menu trees each time you run Quattro Pro, invoke the Menu Tree command and choose the menu file from the list that is offered. Then use the Options–Update command (or the equivalent command on the current menu) to retain this change as the system default.

Startup Macro   Each time you load a spreadsheet, Quattro Pro checks to see if the spreadsheet contains a macro with the special block name specified in the Startup Macro option. If it finds such a name, it will then run that macro. By default, this name is \0 (backslash zero).

OPTIONS–UPDATE

With this command, you save all the current settings on the Quattro Pro menus, thereby making them the default settings for future sessions of Quattro Pro.

The best time to modify system settings and then save them as the defaults is just after you load Quattro Pro. That way, you will know exactly which menu options you have modified and which will therefore be saved as the defaults.

See Also   Graph–Customize Series–Update, Print–Graph Print–Layout–Update, Print–Layout–Update

OPTIONS–VALUES
Version 3 only

This command displays a list of many of the current Quattro Pro 3 settings and their associated values. It shows you at a glance what you would otherwise have to find by calling up several menus. It is a good idea to use the Options–Values command to see the defaults before you invoke the Options–Update command to save them.

OPTIONS–WYSIWYG ZOOM %
Version 3 only

By default, this Quattro Pro 3 option is set to 100 percent, so that fonts appear pretty much as they will when printed. You can set this option as low as 25 percent to reduce fonts to a quarter of their original size, or 200 percent to double the size of all fonts on screen.

If you have set the Options–Graphics Quality command to Final, Quattro Pro will need to access a different screen font each time you adjust the size of the display with the WYSIWYG Zoom % command. If the font does not already exist on disk, Quattro Pro will have to build it. Therefore, you should work in Draft mode when you experiment with different zoom factors, and change to Final mode only when you settle on a satisfactory zoom percent.

PRINT–ADJUST PRINTER

With this command, you can advance the paper in the printer and tell Quattro Pro that you have manually set the paper to a new page.

To Advance the Paper in the Printer

1. From the Ready mode, select **Print** and then **Adjust Printer**.

2. Select **Skip Line** to advance the paper in the printer a single line. You can send as many line feeds as you wish. Or, select **Form Feed** to advance the paper to the next page. You can send more than one form feed if you wish.

To Reset Quattro Pro's Line Count

- From the Ready mode, select **Print**, then **Adjust Printer**, and then **Align**.

• **NOTES** Using the Skip Line and Form Feed commands to control the page position in your printer is both easier and more accurate than adjusting the printer manually, as it lets Quattro Pro know exactly where the next line will print. This ensures that the next print job will paginate correctly. When you must adjust the printer manually, use Align to tell Quattro Pro that there is a new page in the printer. You should also use Align before printing a new report, so that page numbering will begin at page one.

PRINT–BLOCK

In Quattro Pro, you specify the exact block you wish to print. Once you have printed a block, you can specify another block to print, and more if you so choose. Quattro Pro will paginate the printout as needed.

To Specify a Block to Print

1. From the Ready mode, select **Print** and then **Block**.
2. Specify the block you wish to print, then press ↵.

• **NOTES** As with most Quattro Pro commands, the block you print can be in the current spreadsheet or in any other spreadsheet in memory. Include only the rows and columns that you want to print. If the block is too wide to fit within the margins of the page, Quattro Pro will print the remaining columns on subsequent pages, after all the rows of the first portion of the block are printed. If any long text entries in cells within the print block overhang the last column of the block, expand the block to include enough extra columns so that all the text is included in your printout.

See Also Print–Headings

PRINT–COPIES
Version 3 only

Normally during a print job, Quattro Pro prints one copy. But in Quattro Pro 3, you can use the Print–Copies command to specify as many as 1000 copies.

To Print More than One Copy

1. From the Ready mode, select **Print** and then **Copies**.
2. Enter the number of copies you wish to print, from 1 to 1000, and press ↵.

• **NOTES** If you are printing a multiple-page block, Quattro Pro will print a complete set, and then additional sets, until the number specified have been printed. Page numbering in headers and footers will be reset between copies. This command is reset to 1 after each print job.

See Also Print–Layout–Footer and Header

PRINT–DESTINATION

Once you have set all your print parameters for layout, headings, and so on, you can choose to print your work to one of several destinations.

To Select a Destination for Your Printout

1. From the Ready mode, select **Print** and then **Destination**.

2. Choose the device to which you want to print. That device name will appear on the Print menu next to the Destination command, verifying the intended target.

3. If you choose **File** or **Binary File**, you will be prompted for a file name. Enter a file name, with a path if necessary, and press . If you don't specify a file name extension, Quattro Pro will append .PRN to the name.

- **OPTIONS** The File and Printer options below are available in the Draft Mode Printing section. The other options on the Print–Destination menu fall under the category of Final Quality Printing.

File Sends the output to a text file, often called an ASCII file, that contains only standard PC characters. The data will be formatted as it would be when printed on a plain text printer. There will be blank lines for the top and bottom margins, blank spaces on the left for the left margin, and the header and footer will appear as they should.

Use this command to transfer spreadsheet data to another program, such as a word processor. In such a case, you will generally want to set the Print–Layout–Margins–Left command to **0**, Right to **511**, and the Break Pages command to **No**. This produces a less formatted file that will be easier to format within your word processor.

Printer This is the default destination for your printouts. Both it and the Graphics Printer command print to the same printer. The Printer option provides the fastest printing, but it prints in draft mode with the fewest spreadsheet embellishments and will use only the printer's built-in font. If you have inserted any graphs into the spreadsheet with the Graph–Insert command, they will not be included in the printout when you use Printer as the destination. You would need to choose the Graphics Printer destination.

Binary File Sends the output to a binary (non-text) file that contains every bit and byte that would have been sent to the printer, including all the printer control codes, fonts, and spreadsheet data. The result is a transportable file.

Graphics Printer When you want to print your spreadsheet in the highest quality possible and include any inserted graphs, choose Graphics Printer as the destination. The printout will show all the attributes you have assigned to cells in the spreadsheet, such as fonts, line drawing, and cell shading. The printout will, however, take longer to produce than when you select Printer as the destination.

The ultimate quality of the printout also depends on whether the Options–Graphics Quality command is set to Draft or Final.

Screen Preview This is an excellent way to test your printout before actually sending it to the printer. With this setting, the Spreadsheet Print command will send your spreadsheet print block to the screen, in the exact same format as would have been printed if you had used the Graphics Printer option as the destination. Note that your computer's video must be capable of displaying graphics in Quattro Pro.

When you are viewing your printout on the screen, you can press Escape at any time to return to the spreadsheet and the print menu. While you are in the Screen Preview mode, there are several commands available on the menu at the top of the screen. To access a command, either:

- Press the first letter of the command, such as Z for Zoom.
- Press the slash key to activate the menu, use the cursor to highlight the command, and then press ↵.

- Click on the command with the mouse.

The Screen Preview commands enhance the functionality of the preview:

Help: Brings up the Screen Preview Help system, which you can also get by pressing F1.

Quit: Leaves the preview and returns to the spreadsheet. Pressing Escape has the same effect.

Colors: Switches the screen colors to one of the available color sets. This command has no effect on the final, printed output.

Previous or **Next**: Displays the previous or next page, respectively. You can also use the PgUp and PgDn keys.

Ruler: Imposes a one-inch grid over the page. Invoking the command a second time removes the grid from the screen.

Zoom (+) and **Unzoom** (–): Expand and shrink the page by 200 percent, respectively. You can only zoom twice. To reduce the magnification, choose Unzoom (–).

Guide (Ins): Displays a small image of the page in the upper-right corner of the screen. On that page is superimposed a small box, called the *zoom box*, which represents the portion of the page that you are currently viewing. Use the arrow keys to move the box to a different portion of the page, press , and that portion will be displayed. Or just drag the box with your mouse. To remove the small page and zoom box from the screen, invoke Guide again or press Del.

See Also Options–Graphics Quality, Print–Format–Cell-Formulas, Print–Layout–Margins, Tools–Import

PRINT–FORMAT

Normally, Quattro Pro prints exactly what you see on the screen. With the Print–Format command, you can choose to print a list of the actual cell contents of the print block. This type of printout is helpful for debugging and documenting the spreadsheet.

To Print the Cell Contents of a Block

- From the Ready mode, select **Print**, then **Format**, and then **Cell-Formulas**. Or, to use the default setting and print the display, not the cell contents, choose **As Displayed**.

• **OPTIONS** The two choices on the Format menu are As Displayed and Cell-Formulas.

As Displayed When you use As Displayed, the default setting for the Format command, your printout will be an image of your spreadsheet as it appears on the display. The results of formulas are printed, not the formulas themselves.

Cell-Formulas The Cell-Formulas option prints the block in one long column. Each row shows the contents of one cell, and is essentially what you see on the input line when highlighting that cell. The block is printed row by row.

• **NOTES** Use discretion when specifying the size of the block you wish to print. There will be few occasions when you will want to print the cell contents of an entire spreadsheet.

Instead of printing the cell contents to the printer, it can often be more useful to set the Print–Destination command to **File** and send the output to a text file on disk.

See Also Print–Destination–File, Tools–Import–ASCII Text File

PRINT–GRAPH PRINT

You can print a graph with the commands and options on the Print–Graph Print menu. You can also print a graph by inserting it into the spreadsheet with the Graph–Insert command, and then printing the spreadsheet to the Graphics Printer destination.

To Print the Current Graph

1. From the Ready mode, select **Print** and then **Graph Print**.
2. Specify the various print settings on the menu.
3. When you are ready to print, select **Go**.

- **OPTIONS** The Graph Print menu has its own set of formatting options that are similar to those on the Print menu.

Destination The options under Print–Graph Print–Destination are similar to those under the Print–Destination command:

> **File**: This is equivalent to the Print–Destination–Binary File command. It sends the printed graph output to a file on disk. These graphic files are frequently one-half megabyte in size or larger.
>
> **Graph Printer**: Prints to the printer, which must be capable of printing graphics.
>
> **Screen Preview**: This is equivalent to the Print–Destination–Screen Preview command. You save much time and paper if you test your printouts using Screen Preview before printing the output to Graph Printer.

Go Prints the current graph to the device specified on the Destination menu, using the page layout specified on the Layout menu.

Layout You print just one graph per page, and you use the options on the Print–Graph Print–Layout menu to size and position the graph on the page.
  Dimensions: Choose either Inches or Centimeters.

Height and Width: By default, each is set to 0 inches, which Quattro Pro interprets as meaning that you want the graph to be as big as possible, given the current page size and the left and top margins. You can set the width and height to any dimension that will fit within the page, although the 4:3 Aspect ratio setting also affects the size of your graph.

Left Edge and **Top Edge**: By default, each is set to 0 inches. The left edge of your graph will be at the very edge of the paper, and the top edge of the graph will be at the very top of the paper.

Orientation: Choose either **Portrait** (8½ by 11), the default, or **Landscape** (11 by 8½).

Reset: This sets all options on the Print and Print–Graph Print menus back to their default values.

Update: This saves all options on the Print–Graph Print menu and the Print menu as the system defaults for future sessions in Quattro Pro.

4:3 Aspect: This is set to **Yes**, by default, so that Quattro Pro will always maintain a ratio of 4 to 3 between the graph's width and height. Set 4:3 Aspect to **No** when you want to print a graph to a specific size, realizing that its proportions probably will not be what you normally get. This command also affects the scale of graphs that you insert into the spreadsheet with the Graph–Insert command.

Name   This is equivalent to the Graph–Name–Display command. Use it to make one of your named graphs current.

Write Graph File   You can print to a portable binary file by setting the Destination to **File**. You can create other file types by using the Write Graph File option. Note that this command is equivalent to the Go command in that it will create the graph file as soon as you select it. You will be prompted to enter a file name and if you don't specify a file name extension, Quattro Pro will supply one.

The four file types offered provide a means of transferring a Quattro Pro graph to another program or device:

EPS File: Encapsulated PostScript file.

PIC File: Lotus 1-2-3 compatible file.

Slide EPS: Encapsulated PostScript file for making 35mm slides.

PCX File: PC Paintbrush compatible file; a very popular graphics file format.

See Also Graph–Insert, Graph–Name–Display, Options–Update, Print–Destination, Print–Layout

PRINT–HEADINGS

Normally, the column and row titles of your print block appear on only the first page of a multipage printout. Use the Print–Headings command to choose the rows and columns that you want printed as headings on each page of the printout.

To Specify Column or Row Headings

1. From the Ready mode, select **Print** and then **Headings**.

2. Choose **Left Heading** and specify the columns you want printed on the left side of each page. Or, choose **Top Heading** and specify the rows you want printed on the top of each page.

3. To specify the other headings, choose **Headings** again.

• **NOTES** You must specify a valid block for either of the Headings options, but you do not have to define a block equal to the width (for Top Heading) or depth (for Left Heading) of the block. For example, if you are printing the block A1..Z200, you could define the Top Heading as rows 1 to 3 (A1..A3), the Left Heading as columns A&B (A1..B1), and the print block as C4..Z200.

114 Spreadsheet Operations

- **CAUTION** When you specify columns or rows as print headings, do not include them when you specify the print block. If you do, the headings will print twice on the first page: once as the headings and again as part of the print block.

To eliminate the print headings, use the Print–Layout–Reset–Headings command.

See Also Print–Block, Print–Layout–Footer Header, and Print–Layout–Reset

PRINT-LAYOUT

When you print in Quattro Pro, you specify a single block of a fixed width and depth. But you can control precisely where on the page that block will appear with the settings on this menu. Each has a default value that may be fine for most of your printouts.

To Lay Out the Printed Page

1. From the Ready mode, select **Print** and then **Layout**.
2. Specify the various layout settings on the menu.
3. When you are ready to print, select **Print** and then **Spreadsheet Print**.

- **OPTIONS** Use the options on the Print–Layout menu to define the page layout of the printed block.

Break Pages Normally, the printout is paginated with top and bottom margins and any header and footer you specify. If you set Break Pages to **No**, the block will be printed from one page to the next, without top and bottom margins. This gives you the full 66 lines on a standard page. You can still use the Print–Adjust Printer–Form Feed command. Also, hard page breaks within the print block are recognized and the printout will be divided accordingly.

Dimensions By default, this is set to **Lines/Characters**. Horizontal measurements are made in standard print characters, at ten characters per inch (10 cpi). Vertical measurements are made in standard printer lines, which are counted six lines per inch (6 lpi).

Choose **Inches** or **Centimeters** to work with those units of measure when defining the settings on the Layout menu.

Footer and Header Choose **Header** to define the line of text that is printed below the top margin. Choose **Footer** to define the line of text that is printed before the bottom margin. If you don't define a header or footer, Quattro Pro will print a blank line for each of them.

The body of your print block always begins two lines below the header, and ends two lines above the footer.

You can enter as many as 240 characters, and there are three characters that have special meaning when included in a header or footer:

- |: Text justification
- #: Page number of the report
- @: Current date (according to your computer's clock)

Text in headers and footers is by default left-justified. A single vertical bar centers all the text that follows it, but a second vertical bar right-justifies the remaining text. Entering

Date: @|A Report Title |Page (#)

in a header or footer would produce this printed output on page 2 of the report if the date were June 30, 1992:

Date: 30-Jun-92   A Report Title   Page (2)

Margins The options under the Margins command determine where the block, header, and footer will be printed on the page. The unit of measurement for each is determined by the setting on the Print–Layout–Dimensions menu.

Bottom: The amount of blank space between the footer and the bottom of the paper.

Left: The amount of blank space between the left edge of the paper and each line of the print block.

Page Length: The standard printer line height is 1/6 inch. For 11-inch paper, this equals 66 lines per page, the default setting in Quattro Pro. On most laser printers, however, the maximum number of lines per page is 60, and you should set the Page Length option accordingly.

Right: The maximum length of the printed line, measured from the left edge of the paper. Subtract the left margin setting from the right margin to determine the actual length of the printed line.

Top: The amount of blank space between the top of the paper and the header.

Orientation   Allows you to shift the orientation of the printout by 90 degrees. There are three options on this menu (the Banner option was added in Quattro Pro 3):

Banner (Version 3 only): Similar to landscape orientation, except the width of the printout spans as many pages as needed, as though there was one infinitely wide piece of paper.

Landscape: Refers to a page that is wider than it is tall, such as 11 by 8 1/2-inch paper.

Portrait: Refers to a page that is taller than it is wide, such as standard 8 1/2 by 11-inch paper. This is the default orientation.

In order to print in banner or landscape mode, you must select Graphics Printer as the destination for the printout. You should also change the appropriate page layout settings so that, for example, the Page Length option is appropriate for the dimensions of the paper. For banner-mode printing, you must have a printer that uses continuous-feed paper, as most dot-matrix printers do. Single-sheet printers, such as daisy-wheel and laser printers, cannot be used for banner printing.

When you print in banner mode, Quattro Pro formats the printout without paper width boundaries. Headers and footers are therefore printed just once. You can print, for example, a 60-column spreadsheet showing a 5-year business plan. The printout would appear as one very wide piece of paper, without its columns being split among several pages.

Percent Scaling (Version 3 only) In Quattro Pro 3, use this option to scale your printout so that it looks better or fits better on the page. You must select Graphics Printer with the Print–Destination command. By default, Percent Scaling is set to 100 percent, so that your fonts are printed in the sizes you have specified.

By setting this command to a lower or higher number, from 1 to 1000, your printout will shrink or expand to the specified scale.

This command is similar to the Print–Print to Fit command, but they do not work in conjunction. You must print your work with the Print–Spreadsheet Print command in order for the Percent Scaling command to take effect.

Reset Use this when you want to change some or all print settings back to their default. Choose the options you want to clear, and only those settings will be reset to the default:

All: Resets all options on the Print menu, including those under the Graph Print command.

Headings: Resets the definition of the Left and Top Heading options on the Headings menu.

Layout: Resets all the options on the Print–Layout menu except those on the Print–Graph Print–Layout menu.

Print Block: Clears the setting for the Print–Block command.

Setup String This allows you to send a special control code to the printer when printing begins. Each printer has its own set of commands, which are listed in the printer's reference manual.

You must always begin the code and separate each portion of it from other codes with a backslash (\).

For example, the code Escape 0 instructs an Epson printer to use 8-lpi spacing. You would enter that code, using the ASCII numbers for "Escape" (027) and "0" (048), this way: \027\048.

Note that you can also include setup strings in the spreadsheet by prefacing them with the nonprinting label prefix |.

The codes must be placed in a cell within the first column of the print block. The rest of that row will be ignored when printed, so be sure to place the code in an empty or otherwise unnecessary row.

Update This saves all options on the Print menu and Print–Graph Print menu as the system defaults for future sessions in Quattro Pro. It performs the same function as the Print–Graph Print–Layout–Update command.

Values (Version 3 only) In Quattro Pro 3, a window appears that shows all the current settings for the page layout, including margins, page length, setup string, orientation, and so on. This helpful information shows the settings that are saved when you invoke the Print–Layout–Update command.

See Also Print–Graph Print–Layout

PRINT–PRINT TO FIT
Version 3 only

When a printout spills over onto an extra page, use this command in Quattro Pro 3 instead of Print–Spreadsheet Print. Quattro Pro will adjust the printout's font size and line spacing in order to print the spreadsheet block on a single page, or at least as few pages as possible.

The Print–Destination command must be set to Graphics Printer.

To Scale Your Printout Automatically

1. First, set the margin, page length, and other print options as needed.
2. From the Ready mode, select **Print**, and then **Print to Fit**, and printing will begin.

• **NOTES** The Print to Fit command lets you avoid the otherwise tedious job of adjusting font sizes and page margins to make the entire printout fit on a single page. This command supersedes any value you may have entered in the Print–Layout–Percent Scaling command.

To cancel the print job, press Ctrl-Break. If your printer has a buffer, it may continue to print for a page or two.

See Also Print–Layout–Percent Scaling, Print–Spreadsheet Print

PRINT–SPREADSHEET PRINT

When you have specified all the print settings for the printout, invoke this command to begin printing.

To Print the Chosen Spreadsheet Block

1. First, set all the margin, page length, and other print options as needed.
2. From the Ready mode, select **Print** and then **Spreadsheet Print**, and printing will begin.

• **NOTES** When you invoke this command, the printout will be sent to the device specified on the Print–Destination menu. To cancel the print job, press Ctrl-Break. If your printer has a buffer, it may continue to print for a page or two.

You can also use the Print–Print to Fit command to begin printing. If you want to print a graph, use the Print–Graph Print–Go command.

See Also   Print–Print to Fit, Print–Graph Print–Go

STYLE–ALIGNMENT

With the Style–Alignment command, you can change the justification for occupied cells. By default, text is displayed left-justified and numbers are displayed right-justified.

To Align the Entries in a Block

1. From the Ready mode, select **Style** and then **Alignment**.
2. Select the alignment you want from the menu, either **General**, **Left**, **Right**, or **Center**.
3. Specify the block whose cells you wish to align.

• **NOTES**   When you are creating a text entry, you can specify its alignment within the cell by prefacing it with one of the three label prefixes:

- ' : Left alignment
- " : Right alignment
- ^ : Center alignment

For example, entering ^**Date** centers the word Date in the cell. If you don't specify a label prefix, the text you enter will be aligned according to the global (default) alignment, as specified on the Options–Format–Align Labels command.

You can also use the repeating label prefix, \. Entering *– in a cell fills the display for that cell with the text pattern *–*–*–*–. You can shrink or widen the column and the pattern will simply contract or expand to fill the width of the cell.

Never justify a numeric entry by prefacing it with a label prefix. You would be creating a text entry that could not be used in any arithmetic operations. Align numeric cells with the Style–Alignment command. Note that you will generally want to leave numeric entries right-justified, so that a column of numbers will align along their decimal points.

Once you have changed the justification for a cell with the Style–Alignment command, the style you applied will always affect any numeric entry in that cell. Text entries, however, always revert to the default alignment for the spreadsheet. To reset the alignment of one or more cells, use the Style–Alignment–General command.

See Also Options–Format–Align Labels, Style–Block Size–Set Width, Style–Column Width

STYLE-BLOCK SIZE

The commands on the Style–Block Size menu (Style–Block Width in Quattro Pro 2) operate on more than one column or row. The Set Width and Reset Width commands are equivalent to the single-column commands Column Width and Reset Width on the Style menu. The Auto Width command lets you apply an automatic column width to a block of columns. With the Height command in Quattro Pro 3, you can adjust the height of rows.

To Change the Width of Multiple Columns

1. From the Ready mode, select **Style**, then **Block Size**, and then **Set Width**.
2. Specify the block of columns you wish to adjust.
3. Type in a number, from 1 to 254, or use the ← or → key to shrink or widen the columns. Press ↵ to complete the task.

With a mouse, from the Ready mode select one or more cells in the columns you wish to adjust, and then drag the column letter of one of them to size them all.

To Reset the Width of Multiple Columns

1. From the Ready mode, select **Style**, then **Block Size**, and then **Reset Width**.
2. Specify the block of columns you wish to adjust. The width of those columns will be reset to the default width for the spreadsheet, as specified on the Options–Format–Global Width command.

To Set Column Widths Automatically

1. From the Ready mode, select **Style**, then **Block Size**, and then **Auto Width**. You will be prompted to enter the number of spaces that you want to add to the longest entry in each of the columns you will be adjusting. This number will be used to determine the width of each column.
2. Enter the number of spaces, from 0 to 40, and press ↵.
3. Specify the block of columns you wish to adjust.

• **NOTES** The Auto Width command sets the width of a column so that it equals the longest entry in that column, plus the number of spaces you specify. The determining cell entry could be text or a numeric entry with a format that requires a minimum column width.

If you specify a multirow block of columns, such as C5..H30, the Auto Width command looks in each cell in the block to find the longest entry in each column. That entry determines the width of that column. If you specify a one-row block, such as C5..H5, it will look at the entries in all cells in and below that row.

To Adjust the Height of Rows (Version 3 only)

1. From the Ready mode in Quattro Pro 3, select **Style**, then **Block Size**, then **Height**, and then **Set Row Height**.

Style–Block Size **123**

2. Specify the block of rows you wish to adjust.

3. Type in the new row height, from 1 to 240 points. Or, use the ← or ↑ key to shrink the row heights, or the → or ↓ key to make the row heights larger. Press ↵ to complete the task.

With a mouse, from the Ready mode select one or more cells in the rows you wish to adjust, and then drag the row number of one of them (down to increase, up to decrease) to size them all.

• **NOTES** Row height in Quattro Pro 3 is measured in the same units that are used to describe font size: points. By default, row heights are set to 15 points when Font 1 (the default) is Bitstream Swiss 12-point.

If the spreadsheet is not in graphics (WYSIWYG) mode when you adjust row heights, you will not see a change in the spreadsheet. In graphics mode, the changes will be clearly visible, as they will be when you print your spreadsheet.

There will generally be few times when you need to adjust the height of rows, because Quattro Pro adjusts row heights automatically, according to the largest font that is used in the row.

To Reset the Height of Rows (Version 3 only)

1. From the Ready mode in Quattro Pro 3, select **Style**, then **Block Size**, then **Height**, and then **Reset Row Height**.

2. Specify the block of rows you wish to adjust. The height of those rows will be reset to the default height for the spreadsheet, as determined by the current size of Font 1 on the Style–Font menu.

With a mouse, from the Ready mode, select one or more cells in the rows you wish to reset, and then select the Style–Block Size–Reset Row Height command.

See Also Style–Block Size, Style–Column Width, Style–Font, Style–Reset Width

STYLE–COLUMN WIDTH

To widen or narrow a single column, use the Style–Column Width command (Ctrl-W). You can set the width of a column from 1 to 254 characters. The default column width is 9, based on the Options–Format–Global Width command. Use that command to change the default width for every column in the spreadsheet.

To Change the Width of a Single Column

1. Place the cursor within the column you wish to adjust.

2. From the Ready mode, select **Style** and then **Column Width** (Ctrl-W). You will be prompted to enter the new column width.

3. Type in a number from 1 to 254, or use the ← or → key to shrink or widen the column. Press ↵ to complete the task.

With a mouse, you don't need to use the Style–Column Width command. From the Ready mode, simply point to the column letter in the spreadsheet and drag the column to the appropriate width—right to expand or left to contract. Release the mouse button to complete the task.

- **NOTES** Changing a column's width does not affect the contents of any cells in that column, but it will affect the display for those cells. When you have applied a numeric format to a cell, but the column is not wide enough to display that number, the cell will display only asterisks.

See Also Options–Format–Global Width, Style–Block Size, Style–Reset Width

STYLE-FONT

Quattro Pro can display up to eight different fonts in a spreadsheet. Use the Style–Font command to apply one of the eight fonts to a block, or to change one of the eight to a different font.

To Apply a Font to a Block

1. From the Ready mode, select **Style** and then **Font**.
2. Choose one of the eight fonts from the Font menu.
3. Specify the block of cells whose font you wish to change.

• **NOTES** When you apply a font to a cell, you are actually specifying a font *number*. You can later use the Style–Font–Edit Fonts command to change the font associated with that font number. Any cell that had been assigned that font number would then use the new font. Any cells that have not had a font applied to them are assigned Font 1, the default.

Unless you are using Quattro Pro 3 and the spreadsheet is in WYSIWYG mode, you will not actually see the fonts you have applied. Use the Options–Display Mode command to change the display mode to WYSIWYG. Even if they aren't displayed on the screen, however, the fonts will be printed when you print to the Graphics Printer.

The quality of fonts on the display and in printouts is dependent on the setting for the Options–Graphics Quality command.

To Change a Font on the Font Menu

1. From the Ready mode, select **Style**, then **Font**, and then **Edit Fonts**.
2. Choose the font you wish to change from the list of eight fonts on the Font menu.
3. Specify any of the four font attribute options on the font-editing menu.

- **OPTIONS** There are four options for defining a new font:

  Typeface: The style of the character set, such as Roman, Sans Serif, Bitstream Courier, or Bitstream Dutch.

  Point Size: The size of the characters, measured in points. Depending on the typeface you have chosen, sizes generally range from 6 to 72 points.

  Style: Bold, italic, underlined, or reset (no style).

  Color: The color in which the font will be printed on a color printer. The font colors will be displayed on the screen, as well, when the spreadsheet is in WYSIWYG mode. (Use the Options–Color command to change the color of text on the display.)

- **NOTES** The list of eight fonts is saved with the current spreadsheet, so that the same fonts are available the next time you retrieve the spreadsheet. You can use the Style–Font–Update command to save the current list of fonts as the default for future sessions.

See Also Options–Color, Options–Display Mode, Options–Graphics Quality, Options–Update

STYLE–HIDE COLUMN

You can completely hide one or more columns from view by using the Style–Hide Column–Hide command. You can display one or more hidden columns by using the Style–Hide Column–Expose command.

To Hide or Expose Columns

1. From the Ready mode, select **Style** and then **Hide Column**.
2. Choose either **Hide** or **Expose**.

3. Specify the column or block of columns that you wish to hide or display.

● **NOTES** To hide columns C through F, you could specify any block that includes those columns, such as C5..F5 or C9..F50. Hiding columns C through F would make the spreadsheet appear to skip directly from column B to G.

Even though a column may be hidden, you can still refer to its cells in formulas. If you are pointing while creating a cell reference in a formula, all hidden columns will be temporarily displayed so that you can reference cells in those columns. You might find this flipping back and forth to be distracting, so you may want to delay hiding any columns until you have built most of your spreadsheet.

Most Quattro Pro commands that require you to input a block will also let you access hidden columns (the Print command and the Goto [F5] command are exceptions).

See Also Style–Block Size, Style–Column Width, Style–Reset Width

STYLE–INSERT BREAK

When printing, Quattro Pro normally handles the pagination of your printout. It places the correct margins at each edge of the paper, and divides the print block among as many pages as necessary. The Style–Insert Break command lets you direct Quattro Pro to force a page break at any row in the spreadsheet.

To Create a Page Break

1. Start with the cursor on the row that you want at the top of a new page.
2. From the Ready mode, select **Style** and then **Insert Break**.

- **NOTES**   The Insert Break command creates a new row in the spreadsheet, and inserts the special print command code ¦:: into the current cell of the new row. The broken vertical bar is a nonprinting label prefix. In this code, it precedes two colons, which directs Quattro Pro to skip to a new page when printing.

You must create the code within a cell in the very first column of the block that will be printed; otherwise it will be ignored.

STYLE–LINE DRAWING

The Style–Line Drawing command lets you enhance the look of your spreadsheet by adding single-lined, double-lined, or thick-lined borders to cells. You might use it to draw a horizontal line between a set of column titles and the data beneath them, or to create a grid effect in a block of data by placing lines around all the cells in the block.

To Draw Lines in the Spreadsheet

1. From the Ready mode, select **Style** and then **Line Drawing**.
2. Specify the block of cells that will receive the line drawing.
3. From the Placement menu, indicate where the lines should be drawn (see Options, below).
4. From the Type menu, choose the type of line that should be drawn: **Single, Double,** or **Thick.** Or, choose **None** to erase any line drawing from the specified location in the block.
   The line type you specified will be drawn in the block, according to your choice on the Placement menu. The Placement menu will be displayed again, so that you can choose another placement and line-type for the currently selected block.

5. Continue with another set of line drawing, or choose **Quit** to return to Ready mode.

- **OPTIONS** The Placement menu offers you nine different locations for placing lines:

    All: Outlines every cell in the block.

    Outside: Outlines the outside of the block.

    Top: Draws a line above the top row of the block.

    Bottom: Draws a line below the bottom row of the block.

    Left: Draws a vertical line to the left side of the block.

    Right: Draws a vertical line to the right side of the block.

    Inside: Draws lines within the block, but not the outside edges.

    Horizontal: Draws lines between the rows within the block.

    Vertical: Draws lines between the columns within the block.

- **NOTES** Note that vertical lines diminish the usable width of a column by one space, so that you may have to fine-tune your column widths after line drawing.

To remove all line drawing from any location in a block, choose **All** from the Location menu, and **None** from the Type menu.

When printing a block that was enhanced with line drawing, you must include an extra column to the right and an extra row below the block in order to print the line drawing for the block's last column and row.

See Also Style–Shading

STYLE–NUMERIC FORMAT

By applying a format with the Style–Numeric Format command (Ctrl-F), you can change the way a numeric cell is displayed. Note that although the display of the cell is changed, the contents of the cell are not.

If you don't apply a format to a cell, its display is determined by the global format, as specified with the Options–Format–Numeric Format command. Quattro Pro's default global format is General.

To Format a Numeric Cell

1. From the Ready mode, select **Style** and then **Numeric Format**.
2. Select the format style you want from the menu (see Options, below).
3. For those formats that so request, specify the number of decimal places (from 0 to 15) you want displayed.
4. Specify the block of cells you wish to format.

• **OPTIONS** There are ten format styles available on the Numeric Format menu, plus five for dates and four for time. These are shown in Table II.2. In later versions of Quattro Pro 3, use the Options–International–Negative command to choose whether negative numbers are displayed within parentheses (the default) or preceded by a – sign for the Comma and Currency format styles.

• **CAUTION** When you have formatted a cell with a style that is too wide for the cell's column width, Quattro Pro will display asterisks in place of the number. You must choose another format style or widen the column to fully display the cell's contents.

Although the contents of a formatted cell remains unchanged, its formatting can alter its display, disguising its actual contents. In Figure II.7, an @SUM formula in cell B12 appears to provide an incorrect total of 96 for 10 cells of 10. However, a closer look reveals that the cells have an *actual* value of 9.6, even though their *displayed* value is 10. This difference results from the cells' format—Fixed with 0 decimal places, as indicated on the input line—which

Style–Numeric Format

Table II.2: Quattro Pro Formats for Numeric Display

Numeric Format	Input Line	Actual Display
Fixed	(F2)	1234.56
Scientific	(S2)	1.23E+03
Currency	(C2)	$1,234.56
Comma	(,2)	1,234.56
General	(G)	1234.56
Plus/Minus	(+)	+++++
Percent	(P2)	123456.00%

Date

DD/MMM/YY	(D1)	18-May-03
DD/MMM	(D2)	18-May
MMM/YY	(D3)	May-03
Long Intl.	(D4)	05/18/03
Short Intl.	(D4)	05/18

Date-Time

HH:MM:SS AM/PM	(D6)	01:26:24 PM
HH:MM AM/PM	(D7)	01:26 PM
Long Intl.	(D8)	13:26:24
Short Intl.	(D9)	13:26
Text	(T)	+C4+C5
Hidden	(H)	1234.56

The table shows the numeric formats applied to a cell that contains the number 1234.56. The only exceptions are the Plus/Minus and Text formats, which are for a cell that contains the number 5 and the formula +C4+C5, respectively.

132   Spreadsheet Operations

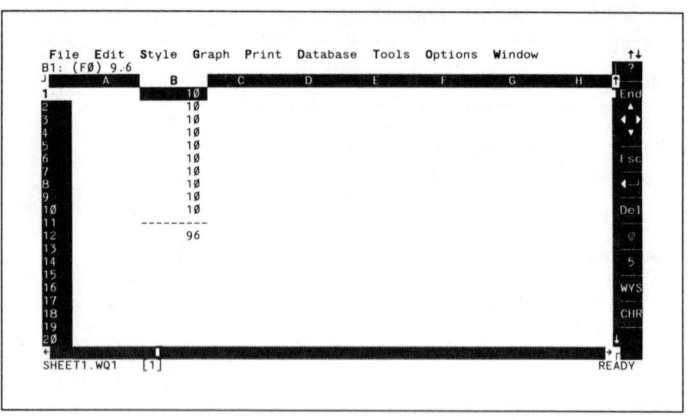

Figure II.7: Numeric formats can disguise the actual cell contents

rounds off displayed numbers to the nearest whole number but leaves the actual cell values intact. In order to correct this problem, you could change the cell format to include one decimal place, re-enter the cell values as whole numbers, or (if the cells contain formulas that reference other cells) use the @ROUND function to round off the actual cell values.

See Also   Options–Format–Numeric Format, Options–International–Negative

STYLE–PROTECTION

You can prevent a block of cells from being changed by protecting them with the Style–Protection–Protect command. By default, all cells in the spreadsheet are initially protected. To unprotect a cell block, use the Style–Protection–Unprotect command. An unprotected cell displays a U on its input line and is displayed in a different color than a protected cell (or in bold on a monochrome system). For a cell's protection status to take effect, however, you must first enable protection with the Options–Protection–Enable command.

To Change a Cell's Protection

1. From the Ready mode, select **Style** and then **Protection**.
2. Choose either **Protect** or **Unprotect.**
3. Specify the block of cells whose protection you wish to change.

• **NOTES**   There are two distinct steps to dealing with cell protection. Whether a cell is protected or unprotected makes no difference if global protection is disabled (the default). To activate the protection status of all cells in the spreadsheet, use the command Options–Protection–Enable. Once enabled, you will not be able to enter data into or change a protected cell.

Once you have enabled global protection, you have two choices available if you need to enter data into a protected cell:

- Unprotect the cell with the Style–Protection–Unprotect command.
- Disable protection on a global basis with the Options–Protection–Disable command.

See Also   Database–Restrict Input, Options–Protection

STYLE–RESET WIDTH

Use the Style–Reset Width command to change the current column's width back to the spreadsheet's default width, as determined by the Options–Formats–Global Width command.

To Reset the Width of a Single Column

1. Place the cursor within the column you wish to reset.
2. From the Ready mode, select **Style** and then **Reset Width**. The column's width will be returned to the global default width.

• **NOTES** When you reset a column's width with the Reset Width command, the input line for cells in that column will no longer display the column's width.

See Also Options–Format–Global Width, Style–Block Size, Style–Column Width

STYLE–SHADING

This command lets you add cell shading to a block to enhance the look of your spreadsheet. For example, you can use shading to call attention to a row of totals or a block of year-end goals.

To Shade a Block of Cells

1. From the Ready mode, select **Style** and then **Shading**.
2. Choose either **Grey** or **Black** from the menu, or choose **None** to erase any cell shading already in the block.
3. Specify the block of cells you wish to shade.

• **NOTES** Cell shading, like numeric formats, line drawing, and other cell attributes, will be duplicated in the target cell when a cell is copied or moved.

See Also Options–Hardware–Printers–Fonts–LaserJet Fonts, Style–Line Drawing

TOOLS–ADVANCED MATH

INVERT

The Invert command returns the inverse value of a square matrix (one with an equal number of rows and columns). You can multiply the result of an inverted matrix by another matrix to effectively divide one matrix by the other.

To Invert a Matrix

1. From the Tools–Advanced Math menu, select **Invert**.
2. Specify the block that contains the square matrix of cells.
3. Specify the upper-left cell of the destination block for the inverted matrix.

MULTIPLY

The Multiply command multiplies two matrices. The first matrix must have the same number of columns as the second matrix has rows. The matrix that is produced by the multiplication will have as many rows as the first matrix and as many columns as the second one.

To Multiply Two Matrices

1. From the Tools–Advanced Math menu, select **Multiply**.
2. Specify the block that contains the first matrix of cells.
3. Specify the block that contains the second matrix of cells.
4. Specify the upper-left cell of the destination block for the resulting matrix of the multiplication.

OPTIMIZATION

Optimization is the process of finding the optimum results based on a set of variables, providing a means for allocating resources among a set of related activities. Quattro Pro's Optimization command is perhaps the most powerful analytical tool in the program; it is certainly the most complex.

To Create an Optimization Model

1. From the Tools–Advanced Math menu, select **Optimization**.

2. Choose **Linear constraint coefficients**, and specify the block that holds the constraint coefficients.

3. Choose **Inequality/equality relation**, and specify the block that holds the operators that denote inequality or equality.

4. Choose **Constant constraint terms**, and specify the column that holds the values that will serve as constraints to the model.

5. Choose **Objective function**, and specify the row of cells that holds the values that will be maximized or minimized.

6. Choose **Extremum**, and choose **Smallest** to minimize the results, or choose **Largest** to maximize them.

7. Choose **Solution**, and specify the cell which will hold the solution of the optimization model.

8. Choose **Variables**, and specify the row of cells which will hold the optimized results of the model.

9. Choose **Go**, and Quattro Pro will calculate the optimal values for the Solution and Variables cells.

- **OPTIONS** You must specify all of the options shown in the steps above in order to define your optimization model. You can also choose these options from the Optimization menu:

   Bounds for Variables: Specify a two-row block with the same number of columns as the Variables block. In the first row, enter the lowest value you will accept for each resulting variable. In the second row, enter the highest value.

Formula Constraints: Instead of specifying the linear constraint coefficients, you can write a constraint formula. Write it so that it logically includes the constant constraint terms and the inequality/equality relations. Quattro Pro will optimize the model so that each formula results in a value greater than zero.

Dual Values: Specify a column containing as many cells as there are constraint coefficients in the input portion of the model. When the model is evaluated, a number will be placed in each cell in this column representing the amount by which the solution cell will change for each increment of 1 to the corresponding constant constraint value.

Additional Dual Values: Specify a row containing as many cells as there are variable cells in the output portion of the model. When the model is evaluated, a number will be placed into each cell in this row that represents the amount by which the solution cell will change for each increment of 1 to either the lower or upper bound for the corresponding variable. This applies only to the bound that limits the resulting variable.

REGRESSION

This command performs a regression analysis on data in your spreadsheet. This is a commonly used method for predicting unknown data based on measured observations. With it, you determine whether or not there is any significant linear correlation between two sets of data.

To Perform a Linear Regression

1. From the Tools–Advanced Math menu, select **Regression**.
2. Choose **Independent** and specify the block that holds the independent variables.
3. Choose **Dependent** and specify the column that holds the dependent variables.
4. Choose **Output Block** and specify the cell where the regression result table should be placed in the spreadsheet.

5. Choose **Go** and the regression analysis will be performed, and the result table created in the specified output block.

● **OPTIONS** The independent data block can be one or more columns of data, as long as there are more rows than columns. The dependent data is always a single column, and it must have the same number of rows as the independent data block.

The Reset command sets all the Regression options to their default values. Normally, Quattro Pro calculates the y intercept (the calculated point at which the y-axis meets the x-axis). Use the Y Intercept command and choose Zero to force the y-axis intercept to zero.

● **NOTES** The regression table in the output block will use nine rows and at least four columns. An extra column will be used for each extra column beyond two in the independent block. It contains the following information:

- Constant: The corresponding y value if x were zero.
- Std Err of Y Est: The standard error of the dependent estimate. The smaller this number, the better the calculated regression values describe the relationship of the data.
- R Squared: The coefficient of determination, it will be a value between 0 and 1. The nearer it is to 1, the more closely related are the independent and dependent data.
- No. of Observations: The number of rows in either of the two blocks of data.
- Degrees of Freedom: The number of observations minus one, minus the number of columns in the independent variables.
- X Coefficient(s): The coefficient of the independent variables.
- Std Err of Coef.: The error factor built into the x coefficient.

TOOLS–COMBINE

The Combine command lets you specify all or a block of another spreadsheet to insert into the current spreadsheet at the cell selector's location. The original spreadsheet remains active, but it now contains data from the second spreadsheet.

Note that you can write linking formulas to perform the same task. But for a large block of data, or data from several different files, the Tools–Combine command may prove faster and require less memory.

To Bring in Cells from a Spreadsheet File

1. First, position the cursor on the cell where you want the data inserted into the spreadsheet.

2. From the Tools menu, select **Combine**.

3. Choose **Add** to add any incoming values to values in the current spreadsheet, choose **Copy** to replace data in cells in the current spreadsheet with the incoming data, or choose **Subtract** to subtract any incoming values from values in the current spreadsheet.

4. Choose **File** to bring in all the cells of another spreadsheet file or, choose **Block** and specify the coordinates or block name of a block in another spreadsheet file.

5. Enter the file name of the spreadsheet from which you want to retrieve data. When you press ↵, the data from that spreadsheet will be brought into the current spreadsheet.

• OPTIONS

Add and Subtract The Add and Subtract options perform arithmetic with the incoming cells and the corresponding cells in the active spreadsheet. With the Add option, an incoming cell is added to the numerical value of the cell it overlays. With the Subtract option, the incoming number is subtracted from the numerical value of the target cell.

The cell in the active spreadsheet must contain a number in order for the addition or subtraction to occur. If the cell contains a formula, text, or a text value, nothing will happen—the incoming cell will be ignored. An incoming cell must contain either a number or a formula that equates to a number; otherwise it, too, will be ignored.

Copy   The Copy option replaces the contents of the cells in the current spreadsheet with the contents of the incoming cells. However, unlike the Edit–Copy command, the Copy option does not replace occupied cells with incoming blank ones. This only applies to entirely blank cells. If the incoming cell has been given a numeric format, for example, that empty but formatted cell will replace a cell in the active spreadsheet.

• CAUTION   Before you bring in an entire file, it is always safest to save your current spreadsheet first. If the incoming file is not the one you wanted, or if the cursor was in the wrong cell when you invoked the Combine command, you can retrieve your spreadsheet and try again. As usual, the Edit–Undo command (Alt-F5) will also undo the problem, as long as you have enabled the Undo feature and use it before making any other changes to the spreadsheet.

See Also   Tools–Import, Tools–Xtract

TOOLS–FREQUENCY

The Tools–Frequency command provides a fast way to create a frequency distribution table. It counts the occurrences of values in a block that fall between a given range of values.

To Create a Frequency Distribution Table

1. Before you begin, you should have created a column of values to serve as the bin block for the frequency distribution table (see Notes).
2. From the Ready mode, select **Tools** and then **Frequency**.

3. Specify the values block that contains the data which you want to count, and then press ↵.

4. Specify the single-column bin block, and then press ↵. The frequency will be calculated and the results placed in the column next to the bin block.

• **NOTES** The bin block you create is a single column of numeric values that you should arrange in ascending order. The Frequency command checks each cell in the values block and finds the first cell in the bin block that is greater than or equal to that value. It then increments the cell to the right of the bin value by one, so that the second column of the bin block shows the results of the frequency distribution.

Any numbers in the values block that are greater than the largest category in the bin block will be counted in the cell below the last number in the bin block.

As you modify your spreadsheet and make changes to entries in the values block, you will have to use the Frequency command again to update the frequency distribution table.

TOOLS-IMPORT

The Import command enables you to import a text file into the spreadsheet. This allows you to access information from a wide variety of other programs, such as documents from a word processor, columns of data collected from a telecommunications session, or data exported to a text file from a database program.

There are three different options on the Import menu that determine how the incoming data will be handled, but the process of using the command remains the same.

To Import a Text File

1. First, position the cursor on the cell where you want the text file to be imported.

142 Spreadsheet Operations

2. From the Ready mode, select **Tools** and then **Import**.

3. Choose one of the three import methods from the menu: **ASCII Text File, Comma & " " Delimited File,** or **Only Commas.**

4. Enter the file name of the text file you want to import. By default, if you don't specify an extension, Quattro Pro will look for file names with a .PRN extension. When you press ↵, the data from the file will be brought into the current spreadsheet.

• **OPTIONS**   There are three different ways to import text into the spreadsheet.

ASCII Text File   Use this option when the text file is not in a columnar format, and need not be broken into distinct columns. Importing a ten-line paragraph from a word processor with this option would create ten cell entries in one column, each as a single long label.

Comma & "" Delimited File   If you intend to perform mathematical or database operations with the incoming data, you will want to break the data into distinct columns. This option will do just that, as long as the data is in an acceptable format. The best format is the one described by the option: each item in a row separated by a comma, with text items enclosed in quotes.

Suppose a text file contains the following line of text:

   1238.56,44.5,"this is text",128892,"More Text"

Importing it into Quattro Pro with the Comma & " " Delimited File option would create five cell entries in a row. The first cell would contain the number 1238.56, the second would contain 44.5, the third cell would be *this is text*, and so on. If all the rows in the text file had the same number of entries, the data would be arranged in perfect columns in the spreadsheet.

Only Commas   Use this option when each item in a row of the incoming text is separated from the next by only a comma. Each item is brought in as a text entry, and there will be no numeric values in the resulting spreadsheet data.

See Also File–Combine, Print–Destination–File, Tools–Parse

TOOLS–MACRO

The options on the Tools–Macros menu help you to write, run, and debug your spreadsheet macros. Note that you can also call up this menu by pressing Alt-F2. See Part VI for more information on writing macros.

CLEAR BREAKPOINTS

When you have set breakpoints in the macro debugger, use this command to clear them all. You can also use the Reset command from within the debugger.

DEBUGGER

The macro debugger helps you test and debug your macros by executing them one step at a time while you view the macro code. Within the debugger, you can set breakpoints in your macros to halt execution at those specified points. You can also view any cells in the spreadsheet and see how their contents change as the macro executes.

To Turn On or Off the Macro Debugger

1. To turn the macro debugger on or off, from the Ready mode, select **Tools**, then **Macro** (Alt-F2), and then **Debugger**.

2. Choose **Yes** to turn on the debugger; you will see the Debug indicator appear on the status line. Or, choose **No** to turn off the macro debugger.

- **OPTIONS**   When the spreadsheet is in Debug mode, the Debug window opens in the lower portion of the screen as soon as you invoke a macro. Macro execution then goes into single-step mode.

You can see the macro code that is being executed in the upper pane of the Debug window. Trace cells are displayed in the lower pane as the macro executes.

The macro executes one step each time you press a key, giving you complete control over the speed of execution. You can also press ↵ to let the macro continue at normal speed, although the spreadsheet will remain in Debug mode.

You access the Debug menu by pressing the slash key, /, while you are executing a macro in Debug mode. The menu offers several options for testing your macros:

Abort: Stops the macro as though you had pressed Ctrl-Break to cancel it.

Breakpoints: Lets you set four regular breakpoints within a macro. When you later run the macro from the debugger, you can press ↵ to let the macro run at full speed. When it reaches a breakpoint within the code, it will shift to single-step mode. You can choose the Pass Count option for a breakpoint and specify the number of passes a looping macro should execute before the breakpoint is invoked.

Conditional: Lets you set four conditional breakpoints within a macro. These breakpoints take effect only when a condition you specify is met. Instead of specifying a line in the macro code as the breakpoint cell, you use any cell in the spreadsheet that contains a logical formula, such as +D21>1400. In this case, when cell D21 contains a value greater than 1400, the macro will pause and go into single-step mode, no matter which line of code was being executed.

Edit a Cell: Lets you change a cell in the middle of macro execution.

Quit: Leave the Debug menu and return to debugging the macro, which you can also do by pressing Escape.

Reset: Clears all macro breakpoints; equivalent to the Tools–Macro–Clear Breakpoints command.

Trace Cells: Lets you specify up to four trace cells, which are cells you wish to watch during macro execution. Those cells will be displayed in the lower debug window.

EXECUTE

With this command, you can invoke the text in any cell as a macro, thereby avoiding the need to give all your macros a keyboard invocable name, such as \A or \G.

To Run a Macro

1. From the Ready mode, select **Tools**, then **Macro**, (Alt-F2) and then **Execute**.

2. Specify the address of the macro you wish to run, or press F3 to bring up the list of all block names in the spreadsheet, and then select a named macro from the list.

After you specify the cell and press ↵, Quattro Pro will execute the macro at that location.

INSTANT REPLAY

This command plays back the macro most recently recorded with the Tools–Macro–Record command. It replays the macro from memory without the need to first copy it into the spreadsheet with the Tools–Macro–Paste command.

KEY READER

This command translates Lotus 1-2-3 macros when they are run under the standard Quattro Pro menu tree. By default, Key Reader is set to **No**, so that a Lotus 1-2-3 macro that accesses the menus will fail when it runs under Quattro Pro's default menu tree. When it is set to **Yes**, 1-2-3 macros will be interpreted as they execute, and will successfully access the Quattro Pro menus.

LIBRARY

With this command, you can designate any spreadsheet as a macro library, so that macros in it can be accessed by any other active spreadsheet. Simply invoke the Tools–Macro–Library–Yes command, and the current spreadsheet will be declared a macro library.

If you have two or more spreadsheets active, and one of them is a macro library, you can invoke macros either in the current spreadsheet or in the library. If the macro name you invoke is not in the current spreadsheet, Quattro Pro will then search the library for the named macro and execute it.

MACRO RECORDING

By default, macros are recorded in the logical, menu-equivalent style, such as { / **Block;Copy**}. If you prefer to record keystroke macros (such as /**ec**), you can use the Tools–Macros–Macro Recording command and choose Keystroke from the menu.

A keystroke macro consists of exactly the same keystrokes that you would use were you to type the commands from the keyboard. Logical macros are much longer than keystroke macros, but the text is more descriptive and therefore easier to interpret. They can also be executed under any menu system in Quattro Pro because they bypass the menus as they run a command.

NAME

This command offers the choices **Create**, for creating a block name, and **Delete**, for deleting a block name. They are equivalent to the two commands of the same name on the Edit–Names menu.

PASTE

When you have recorded a macro with the Tools–Macro–Record command, you can use this command to paste the result into the spreadsheet.

To Paste a Recorded Macro into the Spreadsheet

1. From the Ready mode, select **Tools**, then **Macro** (Alt-F2), and then **Paste**. A list is displayed showing all block names in the spreadsheet.

2. Specify the name of the block where you wish to paste the macro.

3. Specify the block in which the macro should be pasted, if different than the block currently associated with the name.

RECORD

This toggle command switches the spreadsheet in and out of Record mode. When you toggle it on, the Rec indicator appears at the bottom of the screen, and your keystrokes are recorded as you type.

Turn off macro recording by invoking the Record command a second time; the Rec indicator will disappear. You can now either playback the macro with the Tools–Macro–Instant Replay command or copy the macro into the spreadsheet with the Tools–Macro–Paste command.

TRANSCRIPT

The Transcript utility is essentially a macro-recording tool that constantly records your keystrokes in Quattro Pro. It saves all your keystrokes to a file named QUATTRO.LOG in the Quattro Pro subdirectory, providing a history of all your actions in Quattro Pro. This file enables you to rebuild a damaged spreadsheet from any point in the recorded history. You can view the contents of that file by issuing the Tools–Macro–Transcript command.

When you invoke this command, the Transcript window appears. You can scroll the highlight up and down the rows of recorded keystrokes. Press Escape to return to the spreadsheet.

• OPTIONS

Undo Last Command: Replays all keystrokes from the last check point up to, but not including, your most recent keystroke.

Restore To Here: Rebuilds your spreadsheet up to the line in the Transcript history on which you have placed the highlight.

Playback Block: Allows you to specify a block of code in the Transcript window that will be played back as a macro.

Copy Block: Copies the marked block in the Transcript window to the block name you specify.

Begin Block: Marks the current row in the Transcript window as the beginning of a block.

End Block: Marks the current row in the Transcript window as the end of a block.

Max History Length: Lets you change the number of keystrokes retained in the log file. Set this number anywhere between 0 and 25000. Entering zero turns off Transcript's recording.

Single Step: Similar to the macro debugger's single-step mode. When set to **No**, Transcript code is played back at full speed. Choose **Yes**, and the code is executed a step at a time as you press any key. Or choose **Timed**, which inserts a short pause after each keystroke is played before executing the next one.

Failure Protection: By default, Transcript saves your keystroke history to disk after every 100 keystrokes, but you can change this number from 1 to 25000. A value of 1 instructs Transcript to write constantly to disk.

TOOLS–PARSE

When you have imported unformatted, undelimited text into Quattro Pro, each row will contain a long string of characters that are part of a single cell entry. To split each component of a long label into a separate cell, or parse the data, use the Tools–Parse command.

To Split a Long Label into Columns

1. Start with the cursor on the first cell of the text you wish to parse.

Tools–Parse

2. From the Ready mode, select **Tools**, then **Parse**, and then **Create**.

The command inserts a new row, and based on the contents of the first row of data below it, creates a format line. The line specifies how each row of data will be parsed into separate columns (see Options).

You can create other format lines elsewhere in the column of text to define how all following text should be parsed. Each format line must begin with the nonprinting label prefix, !.

3. Choose **Input** and specify the column of text you wish to parse. Be sure to include the format line as the first cell of the block.

4. Choose **Output** and specify the cell where the parsed data should be copied.

5. Choose **Go** to parse the data.

Each line in the input block will be split into separate cells in a row of the output block, based on the layout of the format line.

- **OPTIONS** Use the Reset command to clear all the settings on the Parse menu. The special characters on the format line indicate Quattro Pro's best guess of the type of data that will be parsed:

- D: Recognizable date value
- L: Label
- T: Recognizable time value
- V: Numeric value
- \>: Item continues
- *: Ignores blank spaces
- S: Skips characters below

A date or time in the data must appear in one of the valid Quattro Pro date or time formats, such as 06-Jun-92 or 10:46.

When you use the Edit command to revise a format line, you can scroll the rows below it until a particular row is beneath the format line. You can then revise the format line based on that row.

See Also Tools–Import

TOOLS–REFORMAT

Use this command to reformat a block of text to a width that you specify. It allows you to enter long labels into the cells of a column and then reformat them so that their right margins remain within the same column.

To Reformat a Block of Text

1. From the Ready mode, select **Tools** and then **Reformat**.
2. Specify the block of text you wish to reformat and press ↵.

• **NOTES** When you specify the block, include all the cells in the column that contain the text. Quattro Pro will adjust the length of each line so that it is no wider than the block you specified, wrapping excess text to the next line and adjusting all the other lines in the block.

If you specify a one-row block, all text in contiguous rows below that row will be reformatted. If you specify a multi-row block, Quattro Pro will reformat the text only to the last row in the block. If the block is not deep enough to handle the reformatted text, you will get an error message and the last lines of the block may not be reformatted.

TOOLS–SOLVE FOR

This command lets you solve a mathematical formula "backwards," in the sense that you use the command after you have already set up a mathematical relationship in the spreadsheet.

To Solve a Mathematical Model "Backwards"

1. From the Ready mode, select **Tools** and then **Solve For**.

2. Select **Formula** and specify the cell that contains the key formula.

3. Select **Target Value** and enter the number in which you would like the formula to result. You can also specify a cell address or block name of a cell that contains a value.

4. Select **Variable Cell** and specify the cell containing the value that you want changed so that the formula results in the target value.

5. Select **Go** and a new value will be calculated and placed into the variable cell.

- **OPTIONS**   Use the Reset command to reset each Solve For setting back to its default. You can adjust the depth of the calculation with the two options under the Parameters command:

    Max Iterations: The number of guesses the command should make before it stops calculating, even if it has not come close to an answer. The default is 5; you can specify from 1 to 99.

    Accuracy: The number that represents how close you want the command to get to the target value before it considers the job completed. By default, the amount is 0.005.

TOOLS–UPDATE LINKS

You can write linking formulas that refer to cells in other spreadsheet files. Once a spreadsheet is loaded into memory, you can evaluate its links at any time by using the Tools–Update Links command. While you will rarely need to update formula links if you work on a stand-alone computer, you may need to update all the linking formulas on a regular basis if you work on a network.

- **OPTIONS** Each of the four commands on the Tools–Update Links menu offers you a list of file names that are referenced by any linking formulas in the spreadsheet. You can select any single file name from the list simply by highlighting it and pressing ↵. You can select multiple file names by highlighting each and pressing Shift-F7 or clicking on the name with a mouse. Select all files by pressing Alt-F7.

Change This option enables you to change all occurrences of a file name in all linking formulas in the current spreadsheet. Select the file name you wish to change, and then specify a new file name. The new file name will replace the previous file name in all the linking formulas.

Delete With this command, you can delete all references to a specific file in all linking formulas in the spreadsheet. Select one or more file names from the list, and all formulas that had referenced those files will now reference ERR. You will then need to edit the formulas either to delete the reference or reference another block or file.

Open This option enables you to choose the linked files you wish to load with the spreadsheet. Select one or more files from the list of linked files, and each one will be opened in its own window.

Refresh This option allows you to choose the formula file references you wish to update. Select one or more files from the list of linked files, and any formulas that refer to them will be updated. Note that linking formulas are not updated during normal spreadsheet recalculations, such as when you press the F9 key.

TOOLS–WHAT-IF

This command provides a convenient means for creating a table of calculations without writing formulas for each cell in the table. It derives its name from its ability to help you create and manipulate "what-if" scenarios with your spreadsheet data.

With each of the command's two options, 1 Variable and 2 Variables, you specify a table (block) of spreadsheet data and formulas that are to be used in filling in the interior of the table with the calculated results. The results are based on a single variable cell that you specify for the 1 Variable command, or two cells that you specify for the 2 Variables command.

Figure II.8 shows the structure of both a one-variable and two-variable what-if table.

To Create a One-Variable What-If Table

1. From the Ready mode, select **Tools**, then **What-If**, and then **1 Variable**.

2. Specify the block that contains the what-if table. These are cells A4..E9 in Figure II.8.

3. Specify the input cell for the what-if table (cell F6 in Figure II.8) and the table will be evaluated.

4. Choose **Quit** from the What-If menu to return to Ready mode.

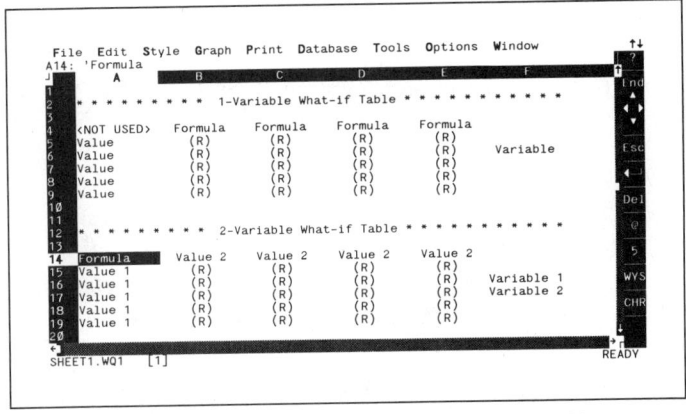

Figure II.8: The layout of a one-variable and two-variables what-if table

154 Spreadsheet Operations

• **NOTES** A one-variable what-if table, such as that in Figure II.8, consists of four components:

- Values: In the one-variable table's first column, cells A5..A9, are the values that you enter as the basis for the calculations. You can use as many rows as you need for the values.

- Formulas: In the table's first row, in cells B4..E4, are the formulas that you enter that will produce the results in the interior of the table, based on the values in the first column. In general, these formulas will refer to the variable cell.

- Variable: The key to the table is a single cell (cell F6 in Figure II.8) that will be used as the variable during calculations. It does not matter what the variable cell contains because its contents will not be used during the calculations. Instead, each value in the first column of the table will be internally substituted into that cell. The formula in each column will then be evaluated, and the result will be placed in each formula's column in the value's row.

- (R): Beneath the formulas row are the results that are produced by evaluating each formula when one of the values in the first column has been substituted into the variable cell.

To Create a Two-Variable What-If Table

1. From the Ready mode, select **Tools**, then **What-If**, and then **2 Variables**.

2. Specify the block that contains the what-if table (cells A14..E19 in Figure II.8).

3. Specify the first input cell for the what-if table (cell F16 in Figure II.8) and then specify the second input cell (cell F17). The table will be evaluated.

4. Choose **Quit** from the What-If menu to return to Ready mode.

• **NOTES** The structure of a two-variable what-if table is shown in Figure II.8. As in a one-variable table, you enter values in the first column. Cells A15..A19 are labeled Value 1 in the figure. But you also enter values in the first row of the table, B14..E14. These are labeled Value 2 in the figure.

Only one formula is used in a two-variable table and it is always placed in the upper-left corner of the table (cell A14 in Figure II.8).

There are always two variable cells associated with the two-variable table, cells F16 and F17 in the figure. Each cell can reside anywhere in the spreadsheet, and just as in a one-variable table, their contents do not affect the results in the table.

When the table is calculated, each Value 1 is placed in Variable 1 and each Value 2 is placed in Variable 2. The formula is evaluated, and the result is placed in the cell at the junction of the two values.

As with the one-variable table, you can use as many rows and columns as you need.

TOOLS–XTRACT

Use the Tools–Xtract command to save a single block of the current spreadsheet to a file. The resulting file retains all the settings of its parent spreadsheet, including the widths of columns, block names, default settings, and cell formats.

To Save a Block to a File

1. From the Ready mode, select **Tools** and then **Xtract**.
2. Choose **Formulas** and any formulas in the block will be saved as formulas, or choose **Values** and only the results of any formulas in the block will be saved.
3. Specify the name of the file to which you want to save a block from the current spreadsheet.
4. Specify the block you wish to save, and that block will be extracted to the file name you specified. If the file already

exists on disk, you will be given the usual file-saving choices Cancel, Replace, and Backup.

• **CAUTION** You must be sure to use a file name that is different from the name of the active spreadsheet, or else you will overwrite the original spreadsheet.

See Also   File–Save, File–Save All, File–Save As, File–Utilities–SQZ!, Tools–Combine

WINDOW–MOVE/SIZE

This command enables you to change the size or position of the current window. You can also move or size a window with your mouse without invoking this command. Note that in Quattro Pro 3, you cannot move or adjust the size of a window when the spreadsheet is in WYSIWYG (graphics) mode.

To Size a Window with the Keyboard

1. From the Ready mode, select **Window** and then **Move/Size** (Ctrl-R). The Move indicator will appear in the upper-left corner of the spreadsheet.
2. Press **Scroll Lock**, and the indicator will change to Size.
3. Use the ← and → keys to narrow or widen the window, or use the ↑ or ↓ keys to shrink or expand the height of the window.
4. Press ↵ to complete the job.

To Move a Window with the Keyboard

1. In order to move the current window, it must be less than full-screen size.

2. From the Ready mode, select **Window** and then **Move/Size** (Ctrl-R). The Move indicator will appear in the upper-left corner of the spreadsheet.

3. Use the ←, →, ↑, or ↓ keys to move the window to a new location on the screen.

4. Press ↵ to complete the job.

• **OPTIONS** After invoking the Move/Size command, you can press any of the following keys to both move and resize the current window to the following positions:

- L: Left half of the screen
- R: Right half of the screen
- T: Top half of the screen
- B: Bottom half of the screen
- Z: Expands the window to full size

To Size a Window with a Mouse

1. From the Ready mode, move the mouse pointer to the resize box, located in the lower-right corner of the spreadsheet, above the mode indicator.

2. Press and hold down the mouse button. The window will be enclosed in a double-lined outline and the Size indicator will appear in the upper-left corner of the spreadsheet.

3. While holding down the mouse button, drag the resize box to the left and up (toward the center of the screen) to shrink the width and height of the window.

4. Move the lower-right corner of the window until the window is the size you want and release the mouse button.

To Move a Window with a Mouse

1. In order to move the current window, it must be less than full-screen size.

2. From the Ready mode, move the mouse pointer to any part of the active window's double-line outline.

3. Press and hold down the mouse button. The Move indicator will appear in the window.

4. Drag the window to a new position on the screen.

5. When the window is where you want it, release the mouse button.

See Also Window–Zoom

WINDOW–OPTIONS

The Window–Options menu contains several commands for manipulating the spreadsheet window.

To Split a Window into Panes

1. Position the cursor on the cell where you want to split the window.

2. From the Ready mode, select **Window**, then **Options**, and then **Horizontal** to split the window horizontally. Or, choose **Vertical** to split the window vertically.

• **OPTIONS** When the window is split, you can move the cell selector from one pane to the other by pressing the Window function key, F6. To move back, press F6 again.

Each pane displays the same spreadsheet, but certain settings affect only the active pane (the one in which the cursor resides). For example, changing the width of a column in one pane will not affect the same column in the other pane. Similarly, changes to the Options–Formats–Numeric Format setting will affect only the active pane.

To return to a single window, use the Window–Options–Clear command. The spreadsheet will revert to the format in effect in the upper or left pane.

Two options affect the way each pane behaves when you scroll through rows or columns.

Sync: By default, the two panes stay synchronized when you scroll. This keeps the columns or rows of each pane aligned as you move through the spreadsheet.

Unsync: Select this option to scroll one pane independently of the other.

To Turn Off or On the Spreadsheet Grid Lines (Version 3 only)

1. From the Ready mode when Quattro Pro 3 is in WYSIWYG (graphics) mode, select **Window**, then **Options**, and then **Grid Lines**.

2. Choose **Display** to turn on the display of grid lines marking the rows and columns of the spreadsheet, or choose **Hide** (the default) to turn off the display.

To Set Locked Titles in the Spreadsheet

1. First, move the cursor to the cell just below or to the right of where you want the locked titles to begin.

2. From the Ready mode, select **Window**, then **Options**, and then **Locked Titles**.

3. Choose **Horizontal** to lock all the rows above the cursor's row, or **Vertical** to lock all the columns to the left of the cursor's column, or **Both** to lock both row and column titles.

• **NOTES** You use the Window–Options–Locked Titles command to lock rows (or columns) at the top (or left side) of the screen. Those rows (or columns) will remain visible even when you scroll the spreadsheet. The locked rows or columns will be highlighted or displayed in a different color.

When writing a formula, you can still point to cells within the locked titles. You can also move to locked cells by using the F5 Goto key.

To View the Spreadsheet in Map View

1. From the Ready mode, select **Window**, then **Options**, and then **Map View**.
2. Choose **Yes**. The spreadsheet display will go into map view.

● **NOTES** This command provides a fast and convenient way to survey a large area of your spreadsheet on one screen. The command has two effects: it shrinks all column widths to one-character width, and it changes the display to reflect the contents of each cell.

Six characters are used to denote the cell contents of each occupied cell:

l	Label (or text)
n	Number
+	Formula
--	Linked formula
c	Circular formula
g	Graph inserted into spreadsheet

By viewing the spreadsheet in map view, it is easy to track down errors, such as formula cells that have been overwritten by numbers.

To Display the Row & Column Borders

1. From the Ready mode, select **Window**, then **Options**, and then **Row & Col Borders**.
2. Choose **Hide** to turn off the display of the spreadsheet row and column identifiers, or choose **Display** (the default) to display them again.

WINDOW-PICK

When you have more than one window open, only one of them is active. The Window–Pick command is one way to access another of the spreadsheet or File Manager windows.

To Make Another Window Active

1. From the Ready mode, select **Window** and then **Pick** (Alt-0). A menu is displayed listing the names and window numbers of all open windows.

2. Highlight the window name you want and press ↵, or click on the window name with your mouse.

- **OPTIONS** There are several other ways to select a window:

  - To reach any of the first nine open windows (those numbered one through nine), simply press Alt and the window number.

  - Press Shift-F6, the Next Window key to activate the next window in line.

  - Press F5, the Goto key, and then type the window's file name, enclosed in square brackets, followed by a cell address or block name, such as [MYFILE]A17.

  - With a mouse, you can activate any window that is visible on the screen simply by clicking on or within its borders.

WINDOW-STACK

The Window–Stack command arranges the windows so that they are overlaid, one on top of the other, like a deck of cards. The window on top is completely in view, although less than full size. The

162 Spreadsheet Operations

windows behind it remain hidden except for each one's top border, showing its name and window number.

When your windows are stacked, using the Shift-F6 key to activate the next window in line is a convenient way to step through the stack, looking at each window in turn.

Note that you cannot use this command in Quattro Pro 3 when the spreadsheet is in WYSIWYG (graphics) mode.

WINDOW–TILE

The command Window–Tile (Ctrl-T) sizes each open window so that all share the screen. If you have just two windows open, this command will place one window on the left side of the screen and the second window on the right. With three windows open, two will share the right side of the screen, and one will occupy the left. With four windows, each will occupy one quadrant of the screen.

This command is available whether the spreadsheet is in text or graphics (WYSIWYG) mode.

WINDOW–ZOOM

When you have sized the current window with the Window–Move/Size command, you can use the Window–Zoom command (Alt-F6) to expand the window back to full size. Once enlarged, you can invoke this command to shrink the window back to its previous size.

If you use the command on a new, full-size window, it will shrink the window to about a half of the screen.

You can also use your mouse to expand or contract a window in one step. Just click on either the ↓ or ↑ in the zoom box in the upper-right corner of the screen.

Part III

The Graph Annotator

The Graph Annotator provides you with several commands for embellishing and modifying your graphs:

- The Pick command enables you to directly modify an entire graph or any of its components.

- The Arrow, Line, Polyline, Polygon, Rectangle and Rounded Rectangle, and Ellipse commands enable you to draw arrows, lines, and shapes in any color or style.

- The Text command enables you to add text anywhere in the graph.

- The Clipboard command enables you to copy portions of a graph to the same or another graph, and import clip-art images to your graphs.

- The Vertical/Horizontal Line command enables you to draw perfect vertical or horizontal lines.

- The Link command enables you to link an object to a data point in the graph, so that the object will move if the data point moves.

These commands are arranged alphabetically after the following introduction to the Graph Annotator.

Accessing the Graph Annotator   To access the Graph Annotator, select the Graph–Annotate command or, when viewing a graph, simply press the slash (/) key.

When you open the Annotator, it automatically displays the current graph. Any changes you make to the graph will remain after you leave the Annotator and return to the spreadsheet.

If you have not defined a graph for the current spreadsheet, the Annotator will display a blank drawing area. Whatever you add here will appear as the current graph in the spreadsheet. Because you

164   The Graph Annotator

have not specified any data, Quattro Pro will set the graph type to Text. A text graph shows only information that has been added through the Annotator.

The Graph Annotator   In Figure III.1, a graph has already been loaded into the Graph Annotator.

In thee graph displayed by the Annotator consists of unique components called *elements*, or *objects*. Each object is either added within the Annotator (such as lines, boxes, text, or images) or loaded into the Annotator with the graph.

Each object has its own set of modifiable *attributes*, or *properties*. The properties for geometric objects include color, pattern, and line style; text properties include typeface, point size, color, and style.

The Graph Annotator consists of five major components: the drawing pad, the drawing toolbox, the property sheet, the gallery, and the status box. Figure III.1 shows a Graph Annotator with a graph already loaded.

The Drawing Pad   The portion of the screen that contains the graph in Figure III.1 is called the *drawing pad*. The boundaries of this

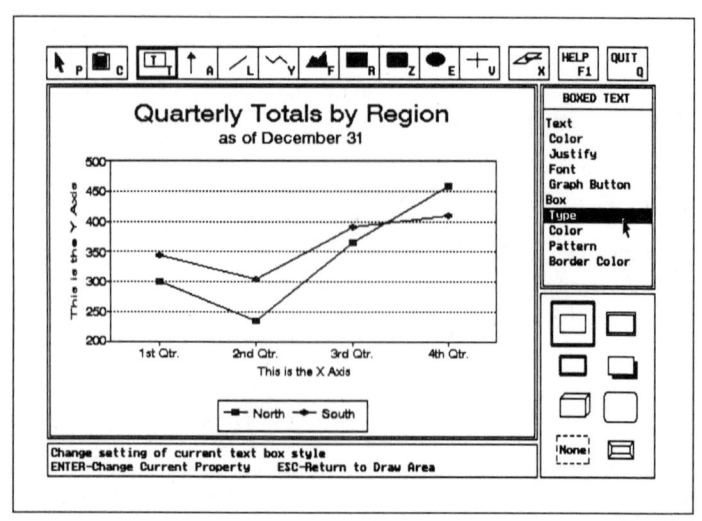

Figure III.1:   The Graph Annotator with a graph to be annotated

area represent the screen boundaries when you view a graph. The arrow below the highlight in the menu on the right is the cursor, or mouse pointer. You don't have to use a mouse in the Annotator, but it is highly recommended.

But you can still move the cursor left, right, up, and down with the ←, →, ↑, and ↓ keys, and you can also move the cursor diagonally with the following keys:

- Home: Up and left
- End: Down and left
- PgUp: Up and right
- PgDn: Down and right

The cursor moves in very tiny increments when you press one of the directional keys. If you need to move the cursor quickly across the drawing pad, press and release the Scroll Lock key before you move the cursor, or press and hold down the Shift key as you move the cursor.

The Drawing Toolbox   The fourteen boxes at the top of the screen in Figure III.1 make up the *toolbox*, or menu. Each box contains a symbol that indicates the command that is invoked when you select that box with the mouse. Each one also contains a letter, which is the letter you type to invoke that command from the keyboard.

The commands on the toolbox are discussed in alphabetical order later in this part.

The Property Sheet   To the right of the drawing pad, just below the toolbox, is the *property sheet*. This small window displays a list of all of the properties for either the currently selected object in the drawing pad or the command you have selected. In Figure III.1, the Text command has been selected, and the list of text properties appears in the property sheet.

To change any of the Text properties with a mouse, just click on the item you want. With the keyboard, use the ↑ or ↓ key to highlight the command you want and then press ↵, or just press the first letter of the command.

When you select a command from the toolbox, the drawing pad remains the active area of the screen. To activate the property sheet, press F3 or use the mouse to click on the property you wish to change. Press Escape to return to the drawing pad.

The Gallery   The *gallery* is the small window below the property sheet. It lists all the choices for the currently selected property. In Figure III.1, the Box–Type property has been selected and the gallery displays the boxes you can choose to enclose text in the graph.

The Status Box   The *status box*, at the bottom of the Annotator screen, displays messages and status reports to remind you of the currently active command or property and what you should do next.

ARROW

Use the Arrow command (A) to draw an arrow in the drawing pad.

To Draw an Arrow

1. Select **Arrow** (A).

2. Position the cursor where you want the arrow to begin. This will be the end opposite the arrowhead.

3. Press the period key, or press and hold down the mouse button to start the arrow.

4. Move the cursor with the arrow keys, or drag the mouse to draw the arrow's shaft.

5. When the line is the correct length, press ↵ or release the mouse button. The arrowhead will appear at the end of the shaft. The color and style of the arrow are determined by the current settings in the property sheet.

• **OPTIONS**   The options for the arrow include Color for the arrowhead, and Color and Style for the arrow's shaft.

CLIPBOARD

The Clipboard (C) command enables you to import and export objects in the drawing pad, as well as shift an object to the foreground or background. Before you can use most of the commands on the Clipboard menu, you must first select one or more objects (see the Pick command).

The Clipboard retains only one set of objects at a time. When you place a new object in the Clipboard, it replaces the previous contents. You can also copy or move one or more objects to a file.

To Cut, Copy, or Paste an Object with the Clipboard

1. Select the object or group of objects that you wish to copy or delete.
2. Select **Clipboard** (C).
3. The property sheet will be activated. Select **Copy** to copy the object to the Clipboard. Select **Cut** to copy the object to the Clipboard and delete it from the drawing pad. Select **Delete** (Del) to delete the object from the drawing pad without copying it to the Clipboard.
4. Select **Paste** to copy the contents of the Clipboard into the drawing pad. You can use the Paste command as many times as you like.

To Cut, Copy, or Paste an Object to or from a File

1. Select the object or group of objects that you wish to copy or delete.
2. Select **Clipboard** (C) and the property sheet will be activated.
3. From the property sheet, select **Copy To** to copy the object to a file, or select **Cut To** to copy the object to a file and delete it from the drawing pad.

4. Enter the name of the file in which you want the object saved. If you do not specify a file name extension, Quattro Pro uses .CLP to denote a clip-art file.

5. You can select **Paste From** at any time to copy the contents of a .CLP file into the drawing pad. You will be prompted for the file name. You can use the Paste From command as many times as you like.

To Change an Object's Position in a Stack

1. Select the object or group of objects that you wish to move to the foreground or background.

2. Select **Clipboard** (C) and the property sheet will be activated.

3. From the property sheet, select **To Top** to move the object in front of other objects, or select **To Bottom** to move the object behind other objects.

ELLIPSE

You can draw an ellipse or a circle with the Ellipse command (E). You create an ellipse in exactly the same way that you create a rectangle (see the Rectangle command), except that the resulting shape will be elliptical, not rectangular.

It is harder to create a circle than an ellipse because you must move the cursor precisely the same vertical and horizontal distance. Before you finish the command, the box you have expanded should be a true square, equal on all sides. This is one instance in the Annotator when the mouse is not the tool of choice.

To Draw an Ellipse

1. Select **Ellipse** (E).

2. Move the cursor to the point where you would like to position one corner of the box that will define the outer tangents of the ellipse.

3. Press the period key, or press and hold down the mouse button.

4. Move the cursor toward the point for the opposite corner of the box. As you move the cursor, an expanding rectangle will appear, with corners at the beginning point and the cursor.

5. When the box is the proper size, press ↵ or release the mouse button, and the ellipse will be drawn within the box.

To Draw a Circle

1. Select **Ellipse** (E).

2. Move the cursor to the point where you would like to position one corner of the square that will define the tangents of the circle.

3. Press the period key.

4. To expand the circle in the vertical plane, count each press of the ↓ or ↑ key as you move the cursor in a vertical direction away from the anchored corner.

5. When you have set the diameter of the circle, press the ← or → key the same number of times to expand the circle in the horizontal plane.

6. Press ↵ to complete the circle.

- **OPTIONS** The properties for Ellipse are Fill and Border, the same as those offered for Polygon (F), Rectangle (R), and Rounded Rectangle (Z). The Fill properties pertain to the inside of the ellipse:

    Color: The color of the fill pattern.

    Pattern: The pattern, or cross-hatching, that will fill the object. Select **No** to leave the ellipse's interior blank.

    Background: The color that will fill the ellipse behind the pattern.

The Border properties of the ellipse include **Color**, **Style**, and **Drawn**. When Drawn is set to **No**, the ellipse will not have a visible border. When it is set to **Yes**, the ellipse's outline will appear according to the Color and Style settings.

HELP

The Help command (F1) opens the help screen for the Graph Annotator, just as pressing F1 brings up help in the spreadsheet or File Manager.

LINE

This command enables you to draw a straight line anywhere in the drawing pad. The drawing process and properties for the line are the same as those for the arrow (see the Arrow command).

LINK

The Link command (X) lets you link an object to a data point in any data series in the graph. That way, when the data in the graph changes, the object will remain connected to that point, even if the point moves to a new position in the graph.

For example, you could link a text box and an arrow to a point on the graph that the text describes. If the position of that data point changes, the text and arrow will continue to point to it.

To Link an Object to a Data Point

1. Select the object in the drawing pad that you want to link to a data point.
2. Select **Link** (X). The property sheet will offer a menu of all six data series, plus the command Unlink.
3. Select the series that contains the data point to which you want to link the object. A dialog box will appear, prompting you to enter the link index for this object.
4. Enter the number of the data point in the series you chose. The first data item in the series is 1, the second is 2, and so on.
5. Press ↵ to complete the task.

To break the link between an object and a data point, select the object and then choose **Unlink** from the Link menu.

PICK

Before you can revise an object in the drawing pad, you must select it. With a mouse, choose the Pick command (P) and then click on an object. From the keyboard, pressing Tab selects a different object in the order in which you created them. Just press Tab until the object you want is selected, or Shift-Tab to select the previous object.

The selected object will have eight little black boxes along its perimeter (except for lines and arrows, which only have two). These are called *handles*, and they remind you that the item has been selected, and can be used to move and resize the object as well. You can also select several items as a *group*.

Once you have selected an object, you can change its position or size in the drawing pad along with any of its properties. The property sheet will reflect the attributes available for the currently selected object. If you press F3 to activate the property sheet and change any of them, the changes will immediately be reflected in the selected object.

To Select an Object

1. From the keyboard, press Tab and the first object in the drawing pad will be selected. Press Tab again to unselect the first and select the second. Repeat this process until the object you want is selected.

2. With a mouse, select **Pick** (P), point to the object you want to select, and click the mouse.

To Select Multiple Objects

1. From the keyboard, just select an object and press Shift-F7 before selecting the next one.

2. With a mouse, position the mouse pointer at one corner of the area you wish to select. Press the mouse button and drag the pointer to the diagonally opposite corner. An expanding rectangle will cover that portion of the screen. Release the mouse button, the rectangle will disappear, and any objects within the rectangle will be selected. If the objects are not in one contiguous area of the drawing pad, press the Scroll Lock key and then click on each object, or hold down the Shift key and then click on each object.

To Align Multiple Objects

1. Select two or more objects in the drawing pad.

2. Select **Align** from the group properties sheet.

3. Specify how you want the objects to align: vertically or horizontally along their sides, their tops or bottoms, or through their centers. The objects will become perfectly aligned.

To Move an Object

1. Select one or more objects.

2. From the keyboard, use the cursor-control keys to move a selected object to the new position. If you selected multiple objects, they will all be moved. Or, with a mouse, point to a spot within a selected object and drag the object to its new position.

To Resize an Object

1. Select one or more objects.

2. With a mouse, drag any of the handles of the selected object to a new position to size that object. If you selected multiple objects, they will all be sized. Or from the keyboard, press the period key to activate the selection handle on the lower-right corner of the object. Move the corner in any direction to size the object. You can make another corner the active one by pressing the period key again.

3. Press ↵ to complete the task.

To Select a Proportional Group of Objects

1. From the keyboard, select multiple objects as described above. Press F7, and the marked objects will be marked as a group—they will lose their individual handles and be enclosed in a single rectangle with handles for the entire group.

2. With a mouse, hold down the Alt key while selecting multiple objects to select the objects as a proportional group.

Once you have a selected a group in this manner, any resizing of the group will be done in proportional manner so that the relative positions of the objects are maintained.

To Set the Attributes for the Background

1. With a mouse, select **Pick** (P) and then click on a portion of the screen outside of the graph. Or, from the keyboard, press Escape and then press /P, and the graph background will be selected.

2. The properties sheet will be labeled Background. Press F3 to activate the properties sheet, and click on a property with your mouse.

3. When you have finished modifying the background, press Escape to return to the drawing pad.

The Graph Annotator

● OPTIONS

Bkg Button You can designate the graph's background to be a graph button. During a graph slide show, if the person at the keyboard or mouse presses any key except a graph-button letter, or clicks on a portion of the graph that is not a button, the graph presentation will end and the user will be returned to the spreadsheet.

You can avoid this problem by setting up a graph background button. Specify the graph you want displayed whenever the person viewing the presentation selects anything in the graph except a defined button. (See also the Graph Button option under the Text command.)

Color This option sets the graph's background color.

Increment This option enables you to adjust the spacing of the drawing pad grid lines, which are spaced according to a percentage of the height and width of the drawing pad (the default is four). You can make the grid lines very tight by lowering the increment (to a minimum of 1), or very loose by raising the increment (to a maximum of 25).

Snap-to This option toggles the drawing pad snap-to effect. When enabled, the edges of objects you create or manipulate are automatically "snapped" to the nearest grid lines on the drawing pad, thereby making it easier to set the alignment of objects. The snap-to effect can be used whether the Visible option is enabled or disabled.

Visible This option toggles the display of the drawing pad grid lines. Setting it to **Yes** displays a grid of dotted lines in the drawing pad, which you can use as a guide for aligning objects.

POLYGON

The Polygon command (F) enables you to draw multisided figures of any shape or size. These objects can be filled with patterns and color.

To draw a polygon, follow the same steps as those for drawing a segmented line with the Polyline command. The difference is that when you finish the object, the last point is automatically connected with the first to close the polygon. The current settings in the property sheet determine the inside color and pattern of the polygon.

Just as with the Polyline command, you can include curved lines in the polygon by pressing the Scroll Lock key or holding down a Shift key as you draw the line.

The properties associated with this command are the same as those associated with the Ellipse command.

POLYLINE

The Polyline (Y) command enables you to draw a line through as many as one thousand points. You can also use this command to draw curved lines if you have a mouse. Although the drawing process is a little different from that of drawing a line or arrow, the Polyline Color and Style properties are the same as those for the Arrow command.

To Draw a Segmented Line

1. Select **Polyline** (Y).
2. Position the cursor at the point where you want the line to begin.
3. Press the period key, or press and hold down the mouse button.
4. Move the cursor to the end point of the line, and press ↵ or release the mouse button.
5. Press ↵ again or double-click the mouse to complete the line. Or, without pressing the period key, move the cursor to the next point you wish to connect with the line and then press ↵. Or, with a mouse, just move the mouse pointer to the next point and click the mouse button.
6. Repeat step 5 for as many segments as you wish to create. The color and style of the line are determined by the current settings in the property sheet.

To Draw a Curved Line

1. Select **Polyline** (Y).
2. Position the mouse pointer at the point where you want the line to begin.
3. Press the Scroll Lock key, or press and hold down a Shift key.
4. Press and hold down the mouse button.
5. Move the mouse pointer in any direction and a curved line will be drawn.
6. To complete the curved line, press Scroll Lock again, or release the Shift key and then release the mouse button. You can mix curved lines and straight segmented lines simply by pressing or releasing the Scroll Lock or Shift key at the appropriate time.

QUIT

The Quit command (Q) returns you to the spreadsheet. The graph on which you had been working is still the current graph, and you can continue to revise it with the options on the Graph menu. If you want to retain any changes you made, be sure to use the spreadsheet's Graph–Name–Create command to name the graph.

RECTANGLE

You can draw rectangles with square or rounded corners by using the Rectangle (R) or Rounded Rectangle (Z) commands, respectively. The properties associated each are the same as those associated with the Ellipse command. To draw a square, follow the steps for drawing a circle, as described under the Ellipse command.

To Draw a Rectangle

1. Select **Rectangle** (R).
2. Move the cursor to the point where you would like to position one corner of the rectangle.
3. Press the period key, or press and hold down the mouse button.
4. Move the cursor toward the point for the opposite corner of the rectangle. As you move the cursor, an expanding rectangle will appear, with corners at the beginning point and the cursor.
5. When the rectangle is the proper size, press ↵ or release the mouse button.

TEXT

You can enter two types of text in a graph: integral text that is part of the graph and free-form text that is entered within the Annotator.

You enter integral text via the Graph–Text menu, using the options 1st Line, 2nd Line, and so on. Once created, this text cannot be changed from within the Annotator. However, you can change the attributes that affect the look of the text, such as its color, its font, or the style of the box that encloses it.

You create free-form text within the Annotator by using the Text (T) command. This text cannot be modified from the Graph–Text menus. It exists as a separate object in the drawing pad.

The quality of text in the Annotator depends on the settings in the spreadsheet's Options–Graphics Quality command.

To Enter Text

1. Select the **Text** (T) command and position the cursor where you want the text to appear.

2. If you want to change any of the text attributes before you begin, press F3 to activate the property sheet, make your selections, and press Escape to return to the drawing pad.

3. Start typing the text, which appears within a box that expands to surround the text as you type.

4. To type a second line of text, press Ctrl-↵ and type the text for that line. Proceed in this fashion for as many lines of text as you need.

5. Press ↵, and the text will be inserted in the drawing pad. By default, the text will be enclosed in a box.

To Edit Existing Text

1. Select the text object you want to edit.
2. Type new text that will replace the existing text, or press F2 to edit the existing text.
3. Press ↵ when finished.

• **OPTIONS**   When you enter text, or have selected a text object, the properties sheet offers several options for changing the look of the text and its surrounding box.

The properties for the box include **Type** (which offers the same box types that are displayed by the spreadsheet's Graph–Overall–Outlines command), **Color**, **Pattern**, and **Border Color**.

The text properties include the following:

Color and Font   Use this command to change the color and font attributes of the text. Its properties offer the same menu of fonts and colors that you see when you use the spreadsheet's Graph–Text–Font command, with one exception. The Annotator's Font–Style–Custom Shadow command offers the choices **Right/Left Drop Shadow** and **Down/Up Drop Shadow**. Entering a number higher than the defaults of 5 and 10, respectively, exaggerates the drop shadow. Entering a negative number switches the drop shadow to the other side of each letter.

Justify   This option specifies how each line of text within the text box will be aligned—either **Left**, **Center**, or **Right** justified.

Graph Button   You can designate a text box to be a graph button, and assign either a named graph or a macro to it. When you later view the graph with the spreadsheet's Graph–View command (F10) or in a slide show, you can either click on the graph button or type the first letter of its text. The graph you assigned to the button will be displayed, or the macro will be run.

You can include slide show transition effects in the definition of the graph button. Just enter any of the five transition descriptions after the graph name and separate each with a semicolon. For example, the button definition

Graph1;20;17;3

will display the graph named Graph1, using transition effect 17 at a speed of 3, for 20 seconds.

To Create a Graph Button

1. Either create a new text entry in the drawing pad or select an existing one. The properties sheet will display the Boxed Text properties.

2. Press F3 to activate the properties sheet and then select **Graph Button,** or click on **Graph Button** with your mouse.

3. You will be prompted to enter a graph name. Type in a name or select one from the list of graph names that is offered (you can include transition effects). Or, type in a macro, of up to 254 characters and press ↵. You can also reference a named macro by enclosing the macro name in brackets.

VERTICAL/HORIZONTAL LINE

The Vertical/Horizontal Line command (V) allows you to draw perfect vertical or horizontal lines, depending on the direction in which you move the cursor. Its Color and Style properties are the same as those for the Arrow and Line commands.

To Draw a Vertical or Horizontal Line

1. Select **Vertical/Horizontal Line** (V).
2. Move the cursor to the point where you want the vertical or horizontal line to begin.
3. Press the period key, or press and hold down the mouse button.
4. To create a vertical line, move the cursor either up or down. Or move the cursor either left or right to create a horizontal line.
5. As soon as you move the cursor, a line will be drawn in that direction. Extend the line to suit your need.
6. Press ↵ or release the mouse button.

Part IV

The File Manager

The File Manager is Quattro Pro's built-in application which helps you manage files on your hard and floppy disks. Although it is not specifically a spreadsheet tool, the File Manager is a most useful feature given Quattro Pro's ability to work with 32 files simultaneously.

Opening a File Manager Window You open a File Manager window by invoking the spreadsheet File–Utilities–File Manager command. In the same way that you can open multiple spreadsheet files, you can open multiple File Manager windows, with each displaying the files on a different drive and subdirectory or even looking at the same location but filtering the file list in a different way.

You can switch to or from a File Manager window in the same way that you would for a spreadsheet window (see the Window–Pick command in Part II).

The File Manager Window Figure IV.1 shows a File Manager window that is currently logged onto the Quattro Pro subdirectory,

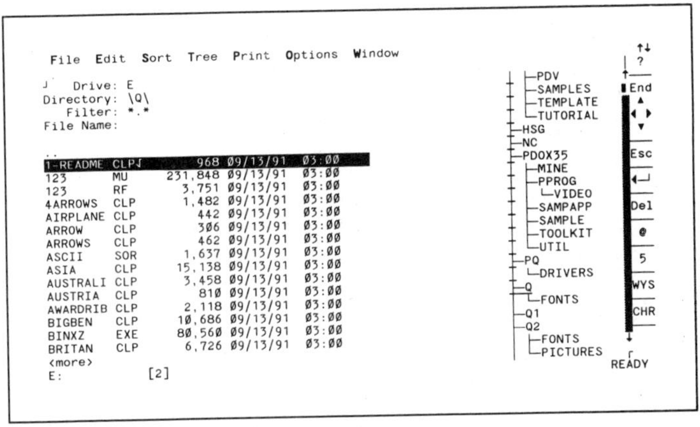

Figure IV.1: A File Manager window

named Q, on the E drive. This example shows all the major components of the window:

- The File Manager menu bar at the top of the screen is similar to the menu bar of a spreadsheet window. The mouse palette is located on the right side of the screen.

- The Control pane, in the upper-left quadrant of the screen, controls where the File Manager looks for files.

- The File List pane, below the Control pane, displays the files in the current location.

- The Tree pane, to the right of the other panes, displays a line-drawing representation of the subdirectory structure of the current drive.

To move the cursor to one of the three panes, press F6, Tab, or click in a pane with your mouse.

The Control Pane You specify the drive and subdirectory to be viewed, as well as the file list filter, in the Control pane. As shown in Figure IV.1, the Control pane contains four settings:

Drive: You can change the drive letter in the Drive option to that of any available disk drive on your system. Nothing happens until you either press ↵ or move the cursor to another item. The File Manager then displays the files in whatever directory is currently active in the specified drive.

Directory: This shows the current subdirectory. You can change to a new one by editing it using the editing keys listed in Table I.1. You can also change to either the parent or a child directory of the current directory simply by picking the appropriate directory name from the File List pane (the name .. always represents the parent directory).

Filter: This determines what file names will be displayed in the File List pane. In Figure IV.1, the filter *.* uses the DOS wildcards that represent any and all characters in the file name and extension, resulting in the display of all files. You can also use the ? wildcard, which represents any single character. Unlike file filters in DOS, you can specify more than one filter by separating them with a comma. For example, to display all files that have a .WQ1 extension as well as all files that have a

.PRN extension, you would use the filter *.WQ1, *.PRN. You can also specify those files that you do not want to see by enclosing the filter within square brackets. For example, specifying [*.WK1] means that no files with a .WK1 extension will be shown.

File Name: When you type a character in this setting, the cursor will jump to the first file name in the File List pane that begins with that character. Type a second character, and the cursor will again move to the first file that begins with both of those characters. In this way, you can search for the file you want in the current subdirectory. You can also include wildcards in the name you type to effect a more general search. If you don't find the file you want in the current directory, you can instruct the File Manager to search for it in all the directories on the current drive by pressing F5.

The File List Pane When the File Manager window is expanded to full size, the list of files in this pane is composed of five columns. From left to right these columns contain the file names, extensions, size, and the date and time of their creation.

By default, the names of subdirectories follow the file names. The first entry is always the twin periods (..) which represent the parent directory of the current subdirectory.

At the bottom of the list of files in Figure IV.1, you can see the word <more>. This indicates that there are more items on the list. You can view more entries on the list by moving the cursor up or down, as follows:

↓ or →	Down one item
↑ or ←	Up one item
PgDn	Down a screen
PgUp	Up a screen
End	End of list
Home	Beginning of list

At the bottom of the file list is a one-line report, such as:

4 of 114 Files 38,597 Bytes Used 4,556,800 Bytes Free

This indicates that there are four entries displayed in the list, out of a total of 114 entries in the current subdirectory; the total number of bytes used by the four files is 38,597; and 4,556,800 bytes are still available on the current drive.

File Manager Commands   Many of the commands on the File Manager's menu are also found on the spreadsheet menu under the same names, such as File–Close, File–New, and Window–Zoom. If a File Manager command is not listed here, refer to the spreadsheet command.

EDIT–COPY

Use this command to copy one or more files from the current directory to another drive or directory. It is equivalent to the DOS command COPY.

To Copy Selected Files

1. First, select the files in the current directory that you wish to copy (see the Edit–Select File command).

2. From the Ready mode, select **Edit** and then **Copy** (Shift-F9). A short beep (or click) will sound, and the marked file names are immediately copied to a hidden area called the paste buffer.

3. With the names waiting in the paste buffer, change to the destination drive or directory, or activate another File Manager window that is logged onto the destination drive.

4. Select **Edit** and then **Paste** (Shift-F10), and each of the files named in the paste buffer will be copied to the new location.

EDIT–DUPLICATE

This command works very much like the DOS command COPY, in that you can rename a file as it is copied. Unlike the Edit–Copy command, Edit–Duplicate works with only one file at a time, and does not use the paste buffer during the duplication process.

To Duplicate a File

1. First, highlight the file in the current directory that you wish to duplicate.

2. From the Ready mode, select **Edit** and then **Duplicate**. You will be prompted to type in the new file name.

3. Enter the new file name and, optionally, a new drive, path, and file extension, and then press ↵.

EDIT–ERASE

Use this command or its shortcut key, Del, to erase one or more files. It is equivalent to the DOS commands ERASE and RMDIR, in that it can also erase empty subdirectories.

To Erase Selected Files

1. First, select the files in the current directory that you wish to erase (see the Edit–Select File command).

2. From the Ready mode, select **Edit** and then **Erase** (Del). A menu will appear with the choices No and Yes. Choose **No** to cancel the command and not erase the files, or choose **Yes** to complete the command and erase the marked files.

188   The File Manager

- **CAUTION**   If you have marked several files, all of them will be erased as soon as you respond with Yes to the confirmation menu. You will not be asked to confirm each deletion. *Do not* accidentally use the Edit–All Select command and then choose Edit–Erase!

EDIT–MOVE

Use this command to move one or more files. It is equivalent to using the DOS command COPY to copy the files to their destination, and then erasing the source files with the DOS commands ERASE or DEL.

To Move Selected Files

1. First, select the files in the current directory that you wish to move (see the Edit–Select File command).

2. From the Ready mode, select **Edit** and then **Move** (Shift-F8). A short beep (or click) will sound, and the marked file names are immediately copied to a hidden area called the paste buffer.

3. With the names waiting in the paste buffer, change to the destination drive or directory, or activate another File Manager window that is logged onto the destination drive.

4. Select **Edit** and then **Paste** (Shift-F10), and each of the files named in the paste buffer will be moved to this location. They will no longer exist in the source directory.

EDIT–PASTE

You use this command or its shortcut, Shift-F10, to complete the process for the Edit–Copy and Edit–Move commands, and copy or move the files from the paste buffer to the current drive and directory.

EDIT–RENAME

This command or its shortcut, F2, is somewhat like the DOS command RENAME, but with a small difference. This command operates on only one file at time, but you can include a new drive and subdirectory in the name, which is equivalent to moving the file to that new location.

To Rename a File

1. First, highlight the file in the current directory that you wish to rename.

2. From the Ready mode, select **Edit** and then **Rename** (F2). You will be prompted to type in the new file name.

3. Enter the new file name and, optionally, a new drive, path, and file extension, and then press ↵.

EDIT–SELECT FILE AND EDIT–ALL SELECT

Many of the commands in the File Manager operate on those files that you have marked (selected) in the file list. A marked file has a small check to the right of its name, and is highlighted in a different color. If you mark an already marked file, it becomes unmarked.

If there is more than one File Manager window open, you can select files in only one window. You can use one of four methods to mark or unmark files:

- If no other files are marked, the file that is currently highlighted in the list is, by default, a marked file.

- Highlight a file and use the Edit–Select File command, or one of its shortcuts, Shift-F7 or the + key.

190 The File Manager

- Click on a file name with your mouse.
- To mark all the files in the list, use the Edit–All Select command (Alt-F7). If one or more files has already been marked, the All Select command will unmark all the files in the list.

FILE–OPEN

This command is the same as the spreadsheet command of the same name. But there is another way to open spreadsheet files from within the File Manager.

To Open the Currently Marked Files

1. If you want to open more than one file, mark their names in the list.

2. Press ↵. If you have marked no other files, the file that is currently highlighted will be opened. Or, if there is more than one marked file, you will be prompted by *Open these documents?*, along with a menu with the choices No and Yes.

4. Choose **No** to cancel the procedure, or choose **Yes** to open all the marked files. This is equivalent to using the File–Open command and specifying each of the marked files in the usual way.

FILE–MAKE DIR

Use this command to create a new subdirectory within the current directory, the one that is shown in the Directory option in the

Control pane. It is equivalent to the DOS command MKDIR. Just as with the DOS command, a directory name can have up to eight characters and its extension can have up to three characters.

To delete a directory, the directory must first be empty of any files or subdirectories. Then use the Edit–Erase command to remove it.

FILE–READ DIR

When you are working in a spreadsheet, F9 serves as the Calc key. In the File Manager, this function key invokes the File–Read Dir command, which performs a similar function. It refreshes the list of files by reading the current disk.

This is especially useful when you are logged onto a floppy disk drive. The File Manager won't know when you put in a new disk, so you must press F9 to have the File Manager read the disk and display the list of files on the new disk.

If you are working on a network, you will need to use the File–Read Dir command periodically in order to update the File Manager's list of files to reflect new activity on the network drive.

OPTIONS–FILE LIST

Use this command to change the display of the File List in the File Manager. By default, the Full View option is in effect. To the right of each file in the list is its file size in bytes and the date and time it was last saved.

To see more file names without the other information, use the Wide View option. This is similar to the /W parameter for the DOS command DIR, which shows you a wide listing of only file names and shows many more file names on the screen.

OPTIONS–STARTUP–DIRECTORY

Each time you open a File Manager window, it reads the file list from the drive and directory specified by the Options–Startup–Directory command on the File Manager menu. This command has two choices, Previous and Current. By default, it is set to Previous, so that the File Manager always looks in the drive and subdirectory that was active during the previous session in the File Manager. If you change the setting to Current, the File Manager will always log onto the drive and directory that are current (the default) when the File Manager is loaded.

If you change the Directory option, you can then use the Options–Update command to retain this new setting for all future sessions in Quattro Pro.

PRINT–BLOCK

The Print menu in the File Manager is similar to the one in the spreadsheet window. However, the Print–Block command offers the choices Files, Tree, or Both, for printing the list of files in the File List pane, the subdirectory tree in the Tree pane, or both of them.

The other choices on the Print menu, such as Page Layout and Destination, affect printouts only from the File Manager.

SORT

By default, the file names in the File List pane are shown in the same order as appear on disk. Use the Sort command to arrange the files by Name, Timestamp, Extension, Size, or DOS Order.

If you were trying to find a spreadsheet you had just created the day before, for example, you could sort by Timestamp so that the newest files would be placed at the bottom of the list.

TREE

The Tree pane displays the entire subdirectory structure for the current disk drive. The root level is at the top, and subdirectories appear down the tree, with each one's subdirectory child subdirectories branching below it to the right. The current directory, as specified in the File Manager's Control pane, will be highlighted in the Tree pane. You can sort the list of subdirectories either by DOS Order or by Name.

• OPTIONS

Close   Removes the Tree pane from the File Manager window.

Open   Opens the Tree pane and displays the directory structure for the current disk. The current subdirectory on that drive will be highlighted in the tree. With the Tree pane displayed, whenever you open a new File Manager window, log onto another disk, or invoke the File–Read Dir command (F9), the File Manager will read the subdirectory structure of the entire disk and draw the tree. This can take some time on a heavily populated disk (perhaps up to 10 or 15 seconds), so you may want to use the Tree pane only when you need it.

Resize   Lets you adjust the size of the Tree pane. The command prompts you to enter a percentage, and then resizes the Tree pane to that percentage of the File Manager window. The default is fifty percent.

• **NOTES** The Tree pane lets you access the subdirectories on the current drive. Instead of typing a new path into the Directory option of the Control pane, you can simply pick the subdirectory you want from the tree.

To access the list in the Tree pane, press F6, Tab, or click in that pane with your mouse. Within the tree, use ↓ or ↑ to move the cursor through the list until you have highlighted the subdirectory you want. To go into a subdirectory to access its own subdirectories, press →. To move back out of a subdirectory to its parent, press ←. As you move to a new subdirectory in the tree, the Directory option in the Control pane and the list of files in the File List pane will reflect the change.

If you have a mouse, and the subdirectory you want is visible on the tree, simply point at it and click the mouse, and that subdirectory becomes the current one.

Part V

@ Functions

A formula in Quattro Pro can be as long as 254 characters and may consist of any of the following parts:

- Value: Numeric (19.5) or string ("hello")
- Cell address: B5, A3..D12, or a block name (THIS_CELL)
- Function: @SUM, @STD, @COUNT, and so on
- Operator: +, –, *, >, =, and so on
- File name: Such as [MYFILE.WQ1], to create a link
- Comments: Optional, separated from the end of the formula with a semicolon

Operators   The glue that joins the numbers, text values, functions, and cell addresses in a formula is the *operators*. Besides the most frequently used operators, such as + (addition), – (subtraction), * (multiplication), and / (division), Quattro Pro provides quite a few others.

Three factors determine the order in which each operation is performed in a formula: its rank in the order of precedence, the use of parentheses, and its position within the formula. The third factor is the simplest. If the other two factors are equivalent (and do not come into play), a formula is evaluated from the left to the right.

By convention, all operators are assigned a rank in the order of precedence. These are listed in Table V.1.

Referencing Cell Addresses   There are several ways to refer to one or more cells in a formula. You can type the address, point to the cell, or use a block name. (For information on defining blocks, see the Introduction to Part II.)

When you copy a formula using the Edit–Copy command, cell references in it adjust their addresses to the copied formula's new location in the spreadsheet. Cell references that change in this manner are called *relative* addresses—the cells to which they point are only relative to the formula's position in the spreadsheet.

When you don't want a cell reference to change when the formula is copied, you can use a reference that is *absolute*. Simply preface its column letter, row number, or both with a dollar sign: +B3. You can copy this formula to any cell in the spreadsheet and it will still refer to B3. For a named block, just preface the name with a dollar sign.

Table V.1 Quattro Pro Operators and Their Order of Precedence

Operator	Description	Precedence
()	Parentheses	8
^	Exponentiation	7
+ −	Positive and negative	6
* /	Multiplication and division	5
+ −	Addition and subtraction	4
=	Equal to	3
>	Greater than	3
<	Less than	3
>=	Greater than or equal to	3
<=	Less than or equal to	3
<>	Not equal to	3
#NOT#	Logical NOT	1
#AND#	Logical AND	1
#OR#	Logical OR	1
&	String concatenation	1

When you are pointing to a cell address while creating a formula, or while editing a formula, you use function key F4 to create an absolute reference to the cell. Press F4 once, and the reference will become absolute (A1, for example). Press it again to make only the row absolute (A$1). You can press it a third time to make just the column absolute ($A1). A fourth press of the F4 key returns the address to its relative state (A1).

A mixed cell reference is one in which you make either the column or row absolute, but not both, as in +$A1 or +A$1.

To make a block reference absolute, precede both of its corner references with a dollar sign: @SUM(A1..G20).

Linking Formulas The ability to work with multiple spreadsheets in Quattro Pro raises the need to reference data in more than one spreadsheet. You do this through the use of linking formulas, which are formulas that refer to cells in other files.

Linking formulas can be as complex as any other formula in the spreadsheet, and can refer to multiple files. The simplest linking formula refers to a single cell in another file. You enclose that spreadsheet's file name in square brackets, and then reference the cell in that file. You would refer to cell A1 in the file named MYWORK as +[MYWORK]A1.

You can write a formula that refers to cells in an active spreadsheet (in memory) or one that resides on disk, so the formula shown above would be valid whether or not the file MYWORK was in memory.

If you are referencing a spreadsheet on a different drive or subdirectory from the current spreadsheet, you must specify the complete path of the referenced spreadsheet, as in +[D:\MYWORK]A1.

You can reference a file either by typing its name into the formula or by pointing to the cells within the spreadsheet, if the file is active in memory. Be sure to include the file name's extension, such as .WK1, if it is different from Quattro Pro's default extension.

You can reference multiple spreadsheet files that have similar names by including wildcards in the file name reference. To sum cell A1 in all files in the current directory that begin with QTR, use the syntax: @SUM([QTR*]A1). The result would look like this if these four files were present:

@SUM([QTR1]A1,[QTR2]A1,[QTR3]A1,[QTR4]A1)

You can create an absolute reference to the cells in another file in the usual way, as in

@SUM([SOMEFILE]A5..B15)

See also the Tools–Update Links command.

Functions   A Quattro Pro *function* is a shortcut for a longer series of calculations. There are 113 functions in Quattro Pro, and each of them begins with the @ symbol and contains a keyword, such as SUM, AVG, or VLOOKUP.

To help you enter functions when you are writing a formula, use the Functions key, Alt-F3. It brings up a menu of all the functions, arranged in alphabetical order. You can scroll through the list until you find the one you want. Highlight that function, press ↵, and it will be placed on the input line as though you had typed it.

In most functions, the keyword is followed by a pair of parentheses. You place one or more parameters within the parentheses; some parameters are required and some are optional.

The parameters for a function fall into these categories:

- Numeric values
- Text values
- Special keyword attributes

You can substitute either a single-cell address, a block of cells, or a block name for any of these parameters. Multiple parameters are always separated by a comma or other delimiter as specified by the spreadsheet's Options–International–Punctuation command; do not include any spaces.

MATHEMATICAL FUNCTIONS

Within this group, the trigonometric functions, such as @SIN and @COS, deal with radians, not degrees. You can use the @DEGREES function to convert from radians to degrees.

@ABS(*n*) The absolute value of *n*, so that the result will always be a positive value. For example,

   @ABS(B9)

returns 15 if cell B9 contains –15 or 15.

@ACOS(*n*) The angle, in radians, that is the arc cosine of *n*, where *n* is a value between –1 and 1. For example,

   @ACOS(0.33)

returns 1.2344, the cosine of which is 0.33.

@ASIN(*n*) The angle, in radians, that is the arc sine of *n*, where *n* is a value between –1 and 1. For example,

   @ASIN(0.75)

returns 0.8481, the sine of which is 0.75.

@ATAN(*n*) The angle, in radians, that is the arc tangent of *n*. For example,

   @ATAN(20)

returns 1.5208, the tangent of which is 20.

@ATAN2(*n,n1*) The arc tangent of the angle determined by the xy coordinates (*n,n1*). For example,

   @DEGREES(@ATAN2(25,25))

results in an angle of 45 degrees since the x and y coordinates are the same.

@COS(*n*)   The cosine of angle *n*. For example,

@COS(@RADIANS(30))

returns 0.8660, the cosine of 30 degrees.

@DEGREES(*n*)   Converts from radians, *n*, to degrees. For example,

@DEGREES(0.7854)

returns 45 degrees.

@EXP(*n*)   The value of e (the mathematical constant) raised to the nth power, or the inverse of a natural logarithm, @LN. If the value of n is greater than 709.8, the function returns ERR because the result would exceed Quattro Pro's range for numeric values: 1.8E+308. For example,

@EXP(7)

returns 1096.63, which is *e* raised to the seventh power.

@INT(*n*)   Truncates any decimal values from *n*, leaving only the integer. For example,

@INT(@PI)

returns 3, which is the integer portion of pi (3.14159).

@LN(*n*)   The natural logarithm of *n*, a value greater than zero, or the inverse of @EXP. For example,

@LN(1096.63)

returns 7, because *e* raised to the seventh power is 1096.63.

@LOG(*n*)   The logarithm of *n*, or 10 raised to the *n*th power. For example,

@LOG(500)

returns 2.6989. Raising 10 to the 2.6989 power (10^2.6989) results in 500.

Mathematical Functions

@MOD(*n,n1*)   Remainder of *n* divided by *n1* (the modulus), where *n* is greater than zero. For example,

   @MOD(18,4)

returns 2, because 18/4 leaves a remainder of 2.

@PI   The value of pi to 13 decimal places: 3.1415926535898.

@RADIANS(*n*)   Converts from degrees, *n*, to radians. For example,

   @SIN(@RADIANS(45))

returns 0.7071, the sine of 45 degrees.

@RAND   Generates a random number between 0 and 1. For example,

   @RAND*(10-1)+1

returns a random number between 1 and 10. To produce a whole number between 1 and 10, see @ROUND.

@ROUND(*n,n1*)   Rounds off *n* to *n1* decimal places. For example,

   @ROUND(28.355,1)

returns 28.4. To round off the integer portion of *n*, use a negative *n1*; for example,

   @ROUND(1429,-1)

returns 1430.

@SIN(*n*)   The sine of angle *n*. For example,

   @SIN(@RADIANS(45))

returns 0.7071, the sine of 45 degrees.

@SQRT(*n*)   The square root of *n*. For example,

   @SQRT(225)

returns 15, and is equivalent to the formula 225^0.5.

@TAN(*n*)   The tangent of angle *n*. For example,

@TAN(@RADIANS(45))

returns 1, which is the tangent of 45 degrees.

STATISTICAL FUNCTIONS

Statistical functions each take a list of numbers or cell addresses as parameters. For example, the @AVG function averages the numbers or the contents of the cells in its list. The list can be written in a variety of forms:

@AVG(B3..D12)
@AVG(B3..D12,C6..C9,F23..I100)
@AVG(16,5,B3..D12)

Most of these functions include a count in their calculation, and you should refer to the warning under the @COUNT function for some problems to avoid.

@AVG(*list*)   The average of the numeric values in *list*. For example,

@AVG(2,4,6,8)

returns 5, the average of the four numbers. Refer to the @COUNT function for a cautionary word on using statistical functions that count.

@COUNT(*list*)   The number of nonblank cells in *list*. For example,

@COUNT(B5..B10)

returns 6 if each cell in the block is occupied. Note that a cell can contain a numeric value or a label, and it will be counted as occupied. Don't include extra cells, such as a dashed line, in the block because those cells will be counted as well.

Referring to a single cell, even if it is blank, will always return a count of 1. To avoid this problem, refer to the cell as a block, and make part of the reference absolute:

@COUNT(2,4,6,8,$A1..A1)

Use the same method with any of the statistical functions that count: @AVG, @STD, @STDS, @VAR, and @VARS.

@MAX(*list*)   The largest numeric value in *list*. For example,

@MAX(A5..B100)

returns the largest value in the block A5..B100.

@MIN(*list*)   The smallest numeric value in *list*. For example,

@MIN(A5..B100)

returns the smallest value in the block A5..B100. If all the other cells contained positive numbers, a cell that was blank or contained a label would cause the result to be 0. Therefore, don't include extra cells, such as a dashed line, in the block being referenced.

@STD(*list*)   The population standard deviation of the numeric values in *list*. For example,

@STD(2,4,6,8)

returns 2.236, which represents the average deviation from the mean of all the values. When all the values are the same, the average will equal any value, and the standard deviation will be zero. Refer to the @COUNT function for a cautionary word on using statistical functions that count.

@STDS(*list*)   The sample standard deviation of the numeric values in *list*. While it is equivalent to @STD, it divides by the number of entries in *list* (the count) minus 1. Refer to the @COUNT function for a cautionary word on using statistical functions that count.

@SUM(*list*)   The total of the numeric values in *list*. This function ignores any blank cells or those with labels in them. For example,

   @SUM(A5..B20,12,C4)

sums all the entries in the block A5..B20, and adds to that total the value 12 and the entry in cell C4.

@SUMPRODUCT(*block1,block2*)   Takes each cell in *block1* and multiplies it by the corresponding cell in *block2*, and then sums all the resulting products. For example,

   @SUMPRODUCT(A1..A5,B1..B5)

returns 130 if the first block contains the numbers 1 through 5 and the second block contains the numbers 6 through 10. It is equivalent to the formula

   @SUM(A1*B1,A2*B2,A3*B3,A4*B4,A5*B5)

@VAR(*list*)   The population variance of the numeric values in *list*. For example,

   @VAR(2,4,6,8)

returns 5. Refer to the @COUNT function for a cautionary word on using statistical functions that count.

@VARS(*list*)   Sample variance of the numeric values in *list*. Equivalent to @VAR, but divides by the number of entries in *list* (the count) minus 1. Refer to the @COUNT function for a cautionary word on using statistical functions that count.

TABLE LOOKUP FUNCTIONS

Table lookup functions return the value of a cell that is found within a block of cells (such as A5..G30) or a list of cells or values (such as B3,C9,6,50,F10) in one of its parameters.

It is important to remember that the columns of the block are referred to in terms of their *offset* from the first column. Therefore, the first column is column 0, the second is 1, and so on.

@CHOOSE(n,list)   The item in *list* in position *n* (the first item in the list is in position 0). For example,

@CHOOSE(@MONTH(@NOW)-1,"Jan","Feb","Mar","Apr", "May","Jun", "Jul","Aug","Sep","Oct","Nov","Dec")

returns *Jul* in the month of July (assuming your computer's internal clock is keeping the correct date and time). This formula is broken into two lines here, but should be written as a single formula. The formula calculates the current month, and then subtracts 1 from it because, as with all lookup functions, the first value in the list has an offset of 0.

@HLOOKUP(x,block,offset)   The horizontal lookup function looks in the first row of *block* for the largest value (or text that matches exactly) that is not greater than *x*, and returns the value found in the cell below it, in the row specified by *offset*. You can use this or the @VLOOKUP function to create tax tables and other numeric lookup tables. Figure V.1 shows a sample tax calculation table. You enter the salary earned (for example, 31500) in B1 (named SALARY) and

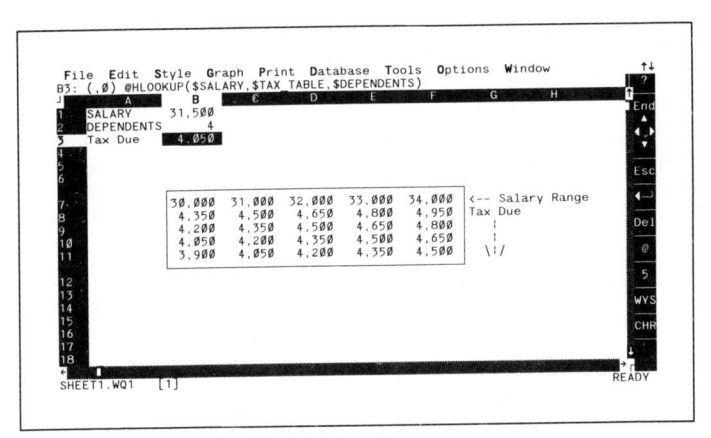

```
 File  Edit  Style  Graph  Print  Database  Tools  Options  Window
B3: (,0) @HLOOKUP($SALARY,$TAX_TABLE,$DEPENDENTS)
        A           B           C         D         E         F         G         H
1   SALARY       31,500
2   DEPENDENTS        4
3   Tax Due       4,050

                    30,000    31,000    32,000    33,000    34,000    <-- Salary Range
                     4,350     4,500     4,650     4,800     4,950    Tax Due
                     4,200     4,350     4,500     4,650     4,800         |
                     4,050     4,200     4,350     4,500     4,650         |
                     3,900     4,050     4,200     4,350     4,500      \!/

SHEET1.WQ1  [1]                                                                READY
```

Figure V.1: The @HLOOKUP function

the number of dependents (for example, 2) in B2 (named DEPENDENTS). The formula in B3,

@HLOOKUP($SALARY,$TAX_TABLE,$DEPENDENTS)

performs the calculation. It looks up the largest salary in the first row (row 0) of TAX_TABLE, B7..F11, that is no greater than the value in SALARY. The formula then looks in that column, for the row with an offset that matches DEPENDENTS, which in this case is row 9 in the spreadsheet. It then results in the value found there, $4,050.

@INDEX(*block,col,row*) Returns the value found in *block* at the junction of *col* and *row*. As usual, the first row and first column of the block have an offset of zero. Unlike @HLOOKUP and @VLOOKUP, which look up a close match in the first row or column of the table, @INDEX looks directly to a specific cell in the table. For example, the formula

@INDEX(PENSION_TABLE,(YEARS_ON_JOB)-1,(CLASS)-1)

would look in the cells named YEARS_ON_ JOB and CLASS, subtract 1 from each of these values (because the first column and row are offset 0, so a value of 1 would look in the first row or column), and then return the appropriate value from the table PENSION_TABLE.)

@VLOOKUP(*x,block,offset*) The vertical lookup function looks in the first column of block for the largest value (or text that matches exactly) that is not greater than x, and returns the value found in the cell to the right of it, in the column specified by offset. This function is essentially the same as @HLOOKUP, but looks across the columns of a table (vertically), not down the rows.

You could rearrange the tax calculation table in Figure V.1 to use @VLOOKUP. You would create the table with the salaries in the first column instead of the first row, and put the taxes due in each column to the right. The first column of taxes due would be for those with one dependent, the second column for two dependents, and so on. The tax calculation function would then be

@VLOOKUP($SALARY,$TAX_TABLE,$DEPENDENTS)

SPREADSHEET INFORMATION FUNCTIONS

The spreadsheet information functions return some type of information about a cell or block of cells. The @CELL, @CELLPOINTER, and @CELLINDEX functions require one of the following *attributes* (enclosed in quotation marks) as part of their parameters:

- *Address*: Cell address
- *Col*: Column number of the cell
- *Contents*: Contents of the cell
- *Format*: Cell's numeric format
- *Prefix*: Label prefix of a text entry
- *Protect*: Cell's protection status
- *Rwidth*: Width, in characters, of a block of cells
- *Row*: Row number of the cell
- *Type*: Type of cell entry
- *Width*: Width of cell's column

@@(*cell*)   The contents of the the cell whose address is specified in *cell*. The @@ function makes an indirect reference to a cell, via the address in *cell*. For example,

@@(A1)

returns 55 when cell F44 contains that value, and cell A1 contains the label F44.

@CELL(*attribute,block*)   The status for the given *attribute* of a single cell or the upper-left cell in block. For example,

@CELL("format",F24)

returns C2 when cell F24 has a Currency format with 2 decimal places.

@CELLINDEX(*attribute,block,col,row*) The status for the given *attribute* of the cell found in *block* at the junction of the column and row. This function is a combination of the @CELL and @INDEX functions. For example,

   @CELLINDEX("row",D40..O122,A1,A2)

returns the row number in the spreadsheet of the cell in the block D40..O122, in the column and row with the offsets shown in cells A1 and A2, respectively. If A1 contains 5 and A2 contains 1, the function would return 41, the row number for cell I41, the row with an offset of 1 in the table.

@CELLPOINTER(*attribute*) The status for the given *attribute* of the cell at the cell selector's location. For example,

   @CELLPOINTER("address")

returns G19 when the cell selector is on that cell. Note that the spreadsheet must recalculate before this function returns the current value for the cell selector's location.

@COLS(*block*) The number of columns in *block*. For example,

   @COLS(A1..F13)

returns 6, because there are six columns in that block.

@ROWS(*block*) The number of rows in *block*. For example,

   @ROWS(A1..F13)

returns 13, because there are 13 rows in that block.

STRING FUNCTIONS

You can't add one string of text to another, but you can *concatenate* them, or join them together. You use the ampersand (&) operator to join two text strings. Because you are creating a formula, the text you join must be enclosed in quotes to indicate that they are text values.

A string formula can also reference a cell that contains either a text value or plain text. If cell A1 contains the text *Thomas*, then the formula

+A1&" Jefferson"

returns *Thomas Jefferson*.

Just remember that all text within the formula must be enclosed in quotation marks. If you mix numeric and text values in the same formula, the formula will result in ERR. You can avoid this problem by using the @STRING and @VALUE functions, which allow you to make a formula either all text or all numeric.

When specifying a character position in a string, the first character has position zero.

@CHAR(n) The ASCII character corresponding to the value of n, where n is a number from 1 to 255. A complete list of all the ASCII characters can be found in Appendix G in the Quattro Pro *User's Guide*. For example,

@CHAR(65)

returns the uppercase letter *A*, because that letter is represented by ASCII number 65. See also the @CODE function.

@CLEAN(s) Removes all nonstandard ASCII characters from string *s*. The nonstandard ASCII characters are numbered 0 through 31. You may find a need for @CLEAN when you have received a text file via a modem, and the text has picked up "garbage" caused by telecommunications static.

@CODE(s) Returns the ASCII code of the first character in the string designated *s*. See also the @CHAR function.

@EXACT(s1,s2) Compares string *s1* with string *s2*, and returns 1 if they are exactly alike or 0 if they are not. The @EXACT function is case sensitive, whereas the expression +*s1*=*s2*, which also compares two strings, is not.

@FIND(*s1,s2,n*)   Returns the position number of the first occurrence of *s1* within *s2*, starting from position *n* in *s2*. For example,

   @FIND("o","Gordon",2)

returns 4, because the first "o" after position 2 is in position 4.

@HEXTONUM(*s*)   Converts the hexadecimal value of string *s* to a decimal value. For example,

   @HEXTONUM("B")

returns 11, which is the decimal value that equals the hexadecimal value B. See also @NUMTOHEX.

@LEFT(*s,n*)   Returns the first *n* characters in string *s*.

@LENGTH(*s*)   Returns the length of string *s*.

@LOWER(*s*)   Converts all letters in string *s* to lowercase.

@MID(*s,n,n1*)   Returns *n1* characters from string *s*, starting with character number *n*. As with all string functions, the first character is number 0. For example,

   @MID("Gordon Shumway",7,4)

returns *Shum*.

@N(*block*)   The numeric value in the cell at the upper-left corner of *block*. For example,

   @N(B14..G40)

returns either the numeric value in cell B14, or zero if B14 does not contain a numeric value.

@NUMTOHEX(*n*)   Converts the numeric value *n* to a string that is the hexadecimal equivalent of *n*. For example,

   @NUMTOHEX(11)

returns *B*, which is the hexadecimal value that equals the decimal value 11. See also @HEXTONUM.

@PROPER(s)   Forces all words in string *s* to initial capitals. For example,

@PROPER("Did you SEE that?")

returns *Did You See That?*.

@REPEAT(s,n)   Creates a string value by repeating *n* times the string *s*. For example,

@REPEAT("XO",5)

returns *XOXOXOXOXO*.

@REPLACE(s1,n1,n2,s2)   Puts string *s2* into string *s1*, replacing *n2* characters, starting at position *n1*. For example, if cell C42 contains "Mrs. Jean O'Riley," the formula

@REPLACE(C42,1,2,"s")

replaces the title Mrs. with Ms.

@RIGHT(s,n)   Returns the last *n* characters in string *s*. For example,

@RIGHT("Gordon",4)

returns *rdon*.

@S(block)   The string value in the cell at the upper-left corner of *block*. Use the @S function to ensure that a formula's reference to a cell will always refer to the string data type. For example,

@EXACT(@S(A1),@S(A2))

will convert numeric values in A1 and A2 to null strings and avoid the ERR result in the @EXACT function.

@STRING(s,n)   Converts the numeric value *n* into a string that looks like the number, and rounds it to *n* decimal places. For example,

@STRING(@PI,2)

returns 3.14.

You can include numeric values in string formulas by converting the numbers into strings with @STRING. For example, the result of the formula

+"The report includes "&@STRING(B5,0)&" data samples."

would be

The report includes 12 data samples.

when B5 contains the number 12.

@TRIM(s)   Removes all leading or trailing spaces and any multiple internal spaces from string *s*. For example,

@TRIM(" So many   spaces!   ")

returns *So many spaces!*.

@UPPER(s)   Converts all letters in string *s* to uppercase. For example,

@UPPER("Did you SEE that?")

returns *DID YOU SEE THAT?*.

@VALUE(s)   Returns the numeric value of string *s*. For example,

@VALUE("$1,234.56")

returns the numeric value 1234.56.

DATE AND TIME FUNCTIONS

To perform date arithmetic in Quattro Pro, you must enter the dates in a form that Quattro Pro can interpret.

Quattro Pro's system of keeping dates is based on a starting date of December 31, 1899. Quattro Pro counts this day as day 1, and numbers each day consecutively after that.

Date and Time Functions

Therefore, to enter the date value for June 1, 1992, you need to count the days from December 31, 1899 to that date and enter the corresponding number, 33756, into a cell. Fortunately, Quattro Pro provides the @DATE function to calculate the date number for you.

You can use a date value to perform date arithmetic. The formula

@DATE(92,6,1)− @DATE(92,1,1)

returns 152, the number of days between January 1 and June 1, 1992.

You can bypass the need for the @DATE function by pressing Ctrl-D, and then typing the date into the cell using one of the five Quattro Pro date format styles. (See the @DATEVALUE reference for a list of the date format styles.) Quattro Pro will automatically convert your entry into a valid date number, and apply the corresponding date format.

To perform time arithmetic, Quattro Pro converts time to a number between 0 and 1, so that 0.5 is 12:00 noon, 0.75 is 6:00 P.M., and 0.9931 is 11:50 P.M. The @TIME function provides an easy way to calculate a time value. Note that Quattro Pro uses 24-hour time in its functions.

@DATE(y,m,d)   Returns the date value for the specified year y, month m, and day d. The year is always expressed as the number of years since 1900, so that 1992 would be entered as 92, and 2011 would be 111. For example,

@DATE(92,6,30)

returns the date number 33785. You can then make the cell appear as a date by applying a date format to the cell with the Style–Numeric Format–Date command.

@DATEVALUE(s)   Returns the date value for the date string s. It is similar to the @TIMEVALUE and @VALUE functions. For example,

@DATEVALUE("6/30/92")

returns the date number 33785. The function requires that the text appear in one of the five Quattro Pro date formats:

- 30-Jun-92
- 30-Jun
- Jun-92
- 06/30/92
- 06/30

@DAY(*n*) The day of the month for the date value *n*. For example,

@DAY(33785)

returns 30, because 33785 is the date value for June 30, 1992.

@HOUR(*n*) The hour for the time value *n*. For example,

@HOUR(33785.75)

returns 18, because 0.75 is the time value for 6:00 P.M., or 18:00 hours in 24-hour time.

@MINUTE(*n*) Returns the number of minutes past the hour for the time value *n*. For example,

@MINUTE(33785.76042)

returns 15, because 0.76042 is the time value for 6:15 P.M.

@MONTH(*n*) Returns the month number for the date value *n*. For example,

@MONTH(33785)

returns 6, because 33785 is the date value for June 30, 1992.

@NOW   Returns the current date and time value as determined by your computer's built-in clock. Entering the @NOW function at 3:00 P.M. on June 30, 1992 returns the date value 33785.625. You could then give that cell a format that displays that value as a date. The displayed date and time are updated when the spreadsheet recalculates.

@SECOND(n)   Calculates the number of seconds past the minute for the time value n. For example,

   @SECOND(33785.76064)

returns 19, because 0.76064 is the time value for 6:15:19 P.M.

@TODAY   Calculates the current date value as determined by your computer's built-in clock, equivalent to @INT(@NOW). Entering @TODAY at 3:00 P.M. on June 30, 1992 returns the date value 33785; there is no time value attached.

@TIME(h,m,s)   Calculates the time value for the specified hour h, minute m, and second s. For example,

   @TIME(18,15,25)

returns the time number 0.760706. You could then format the cell using Style–Numeric Format–Date–Time, so that the time would be displayed as 06:15:25 P.M.

@TIMEVALUE(s)   Calculates the time value for the time string s. This function is similar to the @DATEVALUE and @VALUE functions. For example,

   @TIMEVALUE("6:15 PM")

returns the time value 0.76042. This function requires that the time string appear in one of the four Quattro Pro time formats:

- 06:15:00 P.M.
- 06:15 P.M.
- 18:15:00
- 18:15

@YEAR(*n*)   Returns the year for the date value *n*. For example,

   @YEAR(33785)

returns 92, because 33785 is the date value for June 30, 1992.

FINANCIAL FUNCTIONS

When you are working with one of the financial functions, keep in mind that interest is always expressed as its actual value. Use 0.12 or 12%, not 12, to represent 12 percent. Also, the values for the interest rate and term should always be expressed in relation to the same units. If you are making deposits each month, then your yearly interest rate should be divided by 12 to produce a monthly rate. The term would be the total number of deposits, or 12 in this case.

Quattro Pro has several financial functions that are similar to those in Lotus 1-2-3, but offer enhanced capabilities for the given calculation. These include @FVAL, @IPAYMT, @IRATE, @NPER, @NPV, @PAYMT, @PPAYMT, and @PVAL. These functions offer one or both of the optional parameters *fv* (future value) and *type*. Entering 1 for the *type* parameter specifies that the payment is received at the beginning of each compounding period. Entering a zero, or not using the parameter, specifies that the payment is made at the end of each compounding period.

@CTERM(*int,fv,pv*)   Given the interest rate *int* and present value *pv*, this function returns the number of compounding time periods needed to reach the specified future value *fv*. For example,

   @CTERM(0.12,10000,2000)

returns 14.2, which means it would take a little more than 14 compounding periods to bring the initial investment of $2,000 up to $10,000. If this is a yearly interest rate, then the formula assumes that the interest is compounded annually.

@DDB(*cost,salvage,term,per*) The double-declining balance depreciation of an asset over the number of periods in *term*. For example,

   @DDB(10000,1500,5,1)

returns $4,000, the amount of depreciation allowance at the end of the first year. The amounts for years 2, 3, 4, and 5 are $2,400, $1,440, $660, and 0, respectively. Their total is $8,500, the total difference between the cost and the salvage value.

@FV(*pmt,int,term*) Given regular payments *pmt* and interest rate *int*, this function returns the future value of an investment at the end of *term*. For example,

   @FV(100,0.11/12,5*12)

returns $7,951.81, for a monthly deposit of $100 over five years at an annual rate of 11 percent. See also the @TERM function.

@FVAL(*int,term,pmt,(pv),(type)*) An enhanced version of the future value, @FV function which includes the optional *pv* and *type* parameters. For example,

   @FVAL(0.11/12,5*12,-100,0,1)

returns $8,024.70, for a monthly deposit of $100 over five years at an annual rate of 11 percent. But when you set the optional *type* parameter to 1, the earnings are based on the deposit being made at the beginning of each interest period. (The @FV function, on the other hand, calculates the earnings based on the payment being made at the end of the period.) You can use the optional *pv* parameter if the account contained assets at the start of the term.

@IPAYMT(*int,per,term,pv,(fv),(term)*) Returns the portion of a payment that is interest, not principal. Adding the result of this function with the result of the @PPAYMT function produces the total monthly payment, which should equal the result of the @PAYMT function. For example,

   @IPAYMT(0.11/12,1,30*12,125000)

returns –$1,145.83, which is the interest you pay as part of your first monthly payment on a 30-year loan of $125,000. See also the @PAYMT and @PPAYMT functions.

@IRATE(term,pmt,pv,(fv),(type))   This function is an enhanced version of @RATE that calculates the necessary interest rate to produce *fv* from *pv* over the period in *term*. For example,

   @IRATE(30*12,-1190.40,125000)

returns 0.917%, which is the monthly interest rate (11% annualized) needed to pay off a loan $125,000 over 30 years, with a monthly payment of $1,190.40. Note that the payment must be entered as a negative number. See also the example for @PAYMT.

@IRR(guess,block)   Calculates the internal rate of return of an investment, as specified by the numeric values found in *block*, which represent periodic cash flows (negative values are outflows, positive ones are inflows). The preliminary *guess* is usually not needed, but can serve as a seed for the calculations. For example,

   @IRR(0,A1..A5)

returns 39.06% when the five entries in the block are –1000, 500, 600, 600, and 400.

@NPER(int,pmt,pv,fv,(type))   This function is an enhanced version of @CTERM and @TERM that calculates the number of compounding periods needed to produce *fv* given the interest rate *int*, the payment *pmt*, and a starting balance of *pv*. For example,

   @NPER(0.09/12,100,0,-1200,1)

returns 11.45, the number of compounding periods with equal payments of $100 to reach $1,200 when starting at zero. As usual, a *type* of 1 means that interest is calculated as though the money were transferred at the beginning of each period.

@NPV(int,block,(type))   Calculates the net present value of a future cash flow, as specified by the numeric values found in *block*. For example,

   @NPV(0.09/12,B1..B12,1)

returns $1,152.07 when the cells in the block each contain $100. As usual, a *type* of 1 means that interest is calculated as though the money were transferred at the beginning of each period.

@PAYMT(*int,term,prin,(fv),(type)*)   This function is an updated version of @PMT that offers the optional parameters *fv* and *type*. For example,

   @PAYMT(0.11/12,30*12,125000)

returns –$1,190.40, which is the monthly payment (principal and interest) on a 30-year loan of $125,000.

If the loan will have a balloon payment at the end of *per*, enter the amount for the *fv* parameter.

@PMT(*prin,int,term*)   Calculates the amount of payment due. For example,

   @PMT(125000,0.11/12,30*12)

returns $1,190.40, the monthly payment on a 30-year loan of $125,000 at 11 percent.

@PPAYMT(*int,per,term,pv,(fv),(type)*)   Calculates the portion of a payment that is principal. For example,

   @PPAYMT(0.11/12,1,30*12,125000)

returns –$44.57, which is the principal you are paying as part of your first monthly payment on a 30-year loan of $125,000 at 11 percent. See also the @IPAYMT function.

@PV(*pmt,int,term*)   Returns the present value of regular payments *pmt* and interest rate *int* over the period *term*. For example,

   @PV(1190.40,0.11/12,30*12)

returns $125,000, the present value of making payments of $1,140.40 over 360 periods at 11 percent interest. See also the @PMT function.

@PVAL(*int,term,pmt,(fv),(type)*)   An enhanced version of the present value @PV that includes the optional parameters *fv* and *type*. For example,

   @PVAL(0.11/12,30*12,1190.40)

returns –125,000, the present value of making payments of $1,140.40 over 360 periods at 11 percent interest. See also the @PAYMT function.

@RATE(*fv,pv,term*) Calculates the interest rate needed to produce *fv* from *pv* over the period in *term*. For example,

   @RATE(2000,1000,5)

returns 14.87%, the interest rate needed over 5 periods to compound $1,000 into $2,000. If the interest is compounded monthly, you could write the formula as

   @RATE(2000,1000,5*12)

which returns 1.16%, or an annual rate of 13.94%.

@SLN(*cost,salvage,term*) Calculates the straight-line depreciation of an asset over the number of periods in *term*. For example,

   @SLN(10000,1500,5)

returns $1,700, the amount of depreciation allowance for each of five periods. Multiplying 1700 by 5 returns 8500, the difference between the cost and the salvage value.

@SYD(*cost,salvage,term,per*) Calculates the accelerated depreciation of an asset over the number of periods in *term*. For example,

   @SYD(10000,1500,5,1)

returns $2,833.33, the amount of depreciation allowance for the first year. The amounts for years 2, 3, 4, and 5 are $2,266.67, $1,700.00, $1,133.33, and $566.67, respectively. Their total is $8,500.00, the total difference between the cost and the salvage value.

@TERM(*pmt,int,fv*) Returns the number of payment periods needed to produce *fv* from payments *pmt*, given rate *int*. For example,

   @TERM(100,0.11/12,7951.81)

returns 60, the number of $100 payments it would take at 11 percent interest to reach $7,951.81. See also the @FV function.

LOGICAL FUNCTIONS

Logical formulas can evaluate a complex relationship and return a short answer. The result is either "Yes" or "No," "True" or "False," or in computer talk, "1" or "0." For example, the logical formula 16>10 results in 1, because 16 is greater than 10.

The logical operators provide tools for making logical decisions. You can use the less-than operator, for example, to see if one cell is less than another. You can combine several logical expressions with the #AND#, #OR#, and #NOT# operators. For example,

@IF(C12<C20#AND#C12>C10,F5,G5)

will return the contents of F5 if C12 is less than C20 and greater than C10. Otherwise, G5 will be the result.

@ERR   Returns the value ERR. You will not use this function frequently, but it is a convenient way to force an error condition in formulas. If you are not sure whether a formula refers indirectly to cell A5, for example, enter @ERR into A5 and see if the formula displays ERR.

@FALSE   Returns 0, the logical equivalent of false.

@FILEEXISTS(*filename*)   Returns 1 if the named file is on disk, and 0 if it is not. For example,

@FILEEXISTS("C:\DATA\MYFILE.WQ1")

returns 1 if the file named MYFILE.WQ1 resides in the DATA subdirectory on the C drive. You must include any file extension in order to find the exact file name. Note that the DOS wildcards * and ? can be included in *filename*.

@IF(*cond,true,false*) If the condition *cond* is true, the function returns the *true* statement; otherwise, it returns the *false* statement. For example,

   @IF(A1>B1,A2,B2)

returns the contents of cell A2 if the value of cell A1 is greater than that in B1. If A1 is not greater than B1, then the contents of B2 will be the result.

@ISERR(*x*) Returns 1 if *x* results in ERR; otherwise, it returns 0. You will frequently find a need for this function within @IF formulas that check the status of a cell. For example,

   @IF(@ISERR(A1)=1,A5,A1)

returns the contents of cell A5 if the result in cell A1 is ERR. Otherwise, cell A1 is returned.

@ISNA(*x*) Returns 1 if *x* results in NA; otherwise, it returns 0. This function can serve the same purpose as the @ISERR function, but checks instead for the NA result. See also @NA.

@ISNUMBER(*x*) Returns 1 if *x* is a number; otherwise, it returns 0. Some calculations may perform more reliably if they first check to see that a cell contains a number. For example,

   @IF(@ISNUMBER(A1)=1,A50/A1,A50/A5)

divides A50 by A1 if cell A1 contains a number. If A1 is not a number, the formula will divide A50 by A5.

@ISSTRING(*x*) Returns 1 if *x* is a string; otherwise, it returns 0. This function serves the same purpose as the @ISNUMBER function, but checks instead for strings. For example,

   @IF(@ISSTRING(B30)=1,B30,"No entry in cell B30")

displays the contents of cell B30 if that cell contains a string. If B30 does not contain a string, then the formula will return *No entry in cell B30*.

@NA Always returns NA (not available). This function can serve as a convenient placeholder for a key cell for which you do not yet have a valid entry. Any formulas that refer to the @NA in that cell will result in NA, reminding you that the spreadsheet is not yet complete.

@TRUE Returns 1, the logical equivalent of true.

DATABASE FUNCTIONS

The database functions are enhanced versions of their statistical counterparts. Before you can use these functions effectively, you must know something about the workings of a database in Quattro Pro. See the Database–Query commands in Part II.

Each of these functions performs a different statistical operation on the given data, and all require the same type of parameters and use the same syntax:

@DCOUNT(*block,offset,crit*)

The three parameters include:

- *Block*: A block of cells that can serve as a database input block, and therefore must include a unique title over each column.

- *Offset*: The column on which the function will perform its operation. Columns are counted from the left column of *block*, so that the first column has an offset of 0, the second column is 1, and so on.

- *Crit*: The criteria block that will be used to determine which records in *block* will be included in the calculation.

Look back at Figure II.1, which showed a typical spreadsheet database. The function

@DAVG(A2..G13,6,B17..B18)

would find the average age of all records where the State entry is CA. The formula's parameters refer to the spreadsheet database (A2..G13) and look in the column with an offset of 6 from the left edge of the block (column G). It uses the criterion found in cells B17..B18, which is the same criterion that we used to demonstrate the Database–Query commands. The result would be 35.2, the average of the ages 32, 22, 59, 27, and 36.

Note that spreadsheet recalculation times will slow down drastically when you have many database functions, or just a few that refer to a very large database.

@DAVG(*block,offset,crit*) Returns the average of the selected records' numeric values. See also @AVG.

@DCOUNT(*block,offset,crit*) Returns the number of non-blank cells in the selected records. See also @COUNT.

@DMAX(*block,offset,crit*) Returns the largest numeric value in the selected records. See also @MAX.

@DMIN(*block,offset,crit*) Returns the smallest numeric value in the selected records. See also @MIN.

@DSTD(*block,offset,crit*) Returns the population standard deviation of the selected records' numeric values. See also @STD.

@DSTDS(*block,offset,crit*) Returns the sample standard deviation of the selected records' numeric values. See also @STDS.

@DSUM(*block,offset,crit*) Returns the total of all numeric values in the selected records. See also @SUM.

@DVAR(*block,offset,crit*) Returns the population variance of the selected records' numeric values. See also @VAR.

@DVARS(*block,offset,crit*) Returns the sample variance of the selected records' numeric values. See also @VARS.

SYSTEM FUNCTIONS

The system functions provide information about the current session of Quattro Pro. They are particularly helpful in macros which cannot, for example, look at the Options–Hardware menu to see how much memory is available.

@CURVALUE(*menu,item*)   Returns the current value for a Quattro Pro menu command setting, expressed as a string value, not numeric. This function does not work with some commands, such as Edit–Copy, that have no setting that you can adjust. To reference a menu item, use one of the Quattro Pro menu-equivalent macro commands. For example,

   @CURVALUE("print","leftmargin")

returns 4 when the Left Margin setting is 4.

You will normally use this function within macros when the macro must make a decision based on the current menu settings. For example, a macro might branch to a different print routine if the current graph type is Pie:

   {if @CURVALUE("graph","type")="Pie"}{branch PRINT_PIE}

@MEMAVAIL   Returns the amount of conventional memory that is available. This number will approximate the Bytes Avail setting under the Normal Memory category on the Options–Hardware menu. You could use this and the @MEMEMSAVAIL function in a macro that must first know how much memory is available before it continues with a memory-intensive operation.

   {if @MEMAVAIL<200000}{branch NO_GO}

@MEMEMSAVAIL   The amount of expanded (EMS) memory that is available. This number will approximate the Bytes Avail setting under the EMS Memory category on the Options–Hardware menu. See also the @MEMAVAIL function.

@VERSION   Returns the version number of Quattro Pro.

Part VI

Macro Commands

In the language of computers, a *macro* is a series of actions that can be executed with a single keystroke. In Quattro Pro, macros consist of keystrokes that you could otherwise type from the keyboard, as well as special commands from the macro language. You write a macro simply by writing text (the macro code) into one or more contiguous cells in a column.

Once you have written the text, you can give the first cell in the macro a two-character block name that consists of a backslash and a letter, such as \A or \G, so that you can invoke the macro from the keyboard by pressing Alt and the letter. Or you can use the spreadsheet's Tools–Macro–Execute command to run any macro in the spreadsheet, whether it is named or not.

Once a macro has started, you can cancel it at any time by pressing Ctrl-Break.

Entering Keystrokes A keyboard macro simply plays back recorded keystrokes. You can include codes in your macros to represent such non-character keys on your keyboard as the function keys, cursor-control keys, Home, End, and Escape. You enter these and other codes in curly braces:

{right}	→
{pgup}	PgUp
{home}	Home
{esc}	Escape
{goto}	F5, the GoTo key
{calc}	F9, the Calculate key

The inside cover of this book provides a list of these codes. You can repeat most of these special keys simply by including a space and a number after the keyword, such as {right 2} to move the cursor two cells to the right, or {esc 2} to press the Escape key twice.

Accessing Quattro Pro Menus A macro can access the Quattro Pro menus in two ways—by keystroke or by logical macros. In a keystroke macro, you call the menus simply by using the slash (/) key or the macro keyword {menu}. For example, the macro /fd invokes the spreadsheet's File–Directory command. The problem with accessing the menu in this way is that the macro can fail if it runs under a different menu system from the one in use when you wrote the macro (see the spreadsheet's Tools–Macro–Key Reader command).

Logical macros use "menu-equivalent" commands instead of keystrokes. They execute a specific menu item no matter which menu tree you use. For example, the logical macro that invokes the spreadsheet's File–Directory command, {/ File;Directory}, would work under any menu tree. One problem with menu-equivalent commands, however, is that they require more writing and take up more space in the spreadsheet.

Macro Menus Macro menus behave very much like Quattro Pro's own menus. Each item in a macro menu always consists of three cells in a column:

- First cell: The menu item name, such as View or Print
- Second cell: The descriptive text for the menu item
- Third cell: The actual macro code that will be executed when the menu item is selected

You name the first cell in the first menu item, and that is the name you reference in the {menucall} or {menubranch} commands. The second menu item occupies the three cells in the column to the right of the first item, and any other items fill the columns to the right.

The Need to Use Block Names For all but one-time macros, it is essential that your macros *never* reference a cell by its address. The macro {goto}B10~{right 2} jumps the cursor to cell B10 and moves right two cells. However, a macro, unlike a formula, is just unchanging text in the spreadsheet. This macro, for example, will not perform as you expected if you insert 15 new rows at row 5; it will still jump the cursor to cell B10, but what had been cell B10 will now be cell B25.

To avoid this problem when referencing cells in the spreadsheet, your macros should always refer to block names. In the previous example, if you name cell B10 THAT_CELL and write the macro as {goto}THAT_CELL~{right 2}, the macro will work as planned no matter how you alter the spreadsheet.

The Command Language Syntax The Quattro Pro macro command language has a variety of keywords. When you write a macro, you can use the Macros key, Shift-F3, to call up a complete list of macro keywords. They are presented in this part of the book under the same categories as they appear on the Macros key list.

Many of the macro commands require one or more of the following parameters:

condition   A logical expression that is evaluated as either true or false

col   A column number, usually of a block

item   A numeric or string value, cell address, or block name

location   A cell address or block name

n   A numeric value, a cell address, or a block name that contains a numeric value

prompt   A text message, a cell address, or a block name that contains text

row   A row number, generally of a block

s   A string, a string value, a cell address, or a block name that contains a string or string value

t   The data type, either Value or String

time   The time of day, most often expressed as the current time plus a certain amount of time, such as @NOW+@TIME(0,0,10) to specify 10 seconds from now

SCREEN CONTROL

These macro commands control the screen and sound effects during macro execution. Because they don't affect the spreadsheet, you can add them to your macros as needed.

{beep n}   Instructs the computer to beep using tone n (1-4). If you don't specify a parameter, the macro sets the value of n to 1. For example,

   {beep SOMECELL}

sounds a beep, with a tone based on the value in the cell named SOMECELL.

{indicate s}   Sets the mode indicator to the string s, to a maximum of five characters. You should enclose the text in quotation marks. For example,

   {indicate "VIEW"}

changes the mode indicator to VIEW. Using this command without a parameter returns the mode indicator to its default status.

{paneloff}–{panelon}   This command freezes the display of the menus, input line, and status line until the macro is finished or the {panelon} command is executed. See also the Options–Other–Macro command in Part II.

{windowsoff}–{windowson}   This command freezes the display of the spreadsheet until the macro is finished or the {windowson} command is executed. See also the Options–Other–Macro command in Part II.

USER INTERACTION

These keywords allow your macros to interact with the person behind the keyboard. They can serve to prompt the user to enter information, offer a menu, display a message, and insert a timed pause into a macro.

{?}   This command pauses macro execution until the user presses ↵. Note that the press of the ↵ key is intercepted by this command, and is not passed on to the spreadsheet. For example,

    {message GET_FILE, 20,9,0}
    {/ File;Retrieve}{Clear}{?}~

prompts the user to enter a file to retrieve. It then invokes the File–Retrieve command, clears the dialog box, and waits for the user to type in a file name. When the user presses ↵, the macro continues, in this case with the final ~, which actually "presses" ↵ to retrieve the file. The only indication that the {?} macro is active (although waiting) is the Macro indicator on the status line.

{breakoff}–{breakon}   This command disables the functioning of the Ctrl-Break key. Use this command with extreme caution—you can write a macro that is impossible to cancel.

{get *loc*}   This command pauses and waits for a key to be pressed. The keystroke is stored as a character in *loc*, but is not acted upon by the spreadsheet. Keys such as ↓ and Home are stored as their macro equivalents, {DOWN} and {HOME}.

{getlabel *prompt,loc*}   This command pauses and displays *prompt* in the input line, and then waits for the user to type a response and press ↵. The entry is stored as text in *loc*. *Prompt* can contain up to 70 characters and should be enclosed in quotation marks. You can also use a string formula to refer to a cell address or block name that contains the message. For example,

    {getlabel "Do you want to print? (Y/N)- ",CHOICE}
    {if CHOICE="Y"}{DO_PRINT}

232   Macro Commands

displays the prompt *Do you want to print? (Y/N)–* and waits for input. When ↵ is pressed, the input is stored in the cell named CHOICE. The next line checks CHOICE, and if it contains Y, the macro continues with DO_PRINT.

{getnumber *prompt,loc*}   This command is similar to {getlabel}, but user input is stored as a numeric value. If a nonnumeric entry is made, an ERR result will appear in *loc*. For example,

```
{getnumber "Move down how many rows ?",CHOICE}
{down CHOICE}
```

stores user input as a value in CHOICE, and the next line of the macro moves the cursor down that number of rows.

{graphchar *loc*}   When viewing a graph or a message with the {message} macro, this command captures the keystroke that the user presses to return to the spreadsheet. For example,

```
{message MESSAGE1,30,10,0}
{graphchar CHOICE}
{if CHOICE="Y"}{branch SOME_MORE}
{if CHOICE="N"}{branch NO_MORE}
{branch ASK_AGAIN}
```

displays a message box and waits for the user to press a key. The {graphchar} command captures that keystroke and stores it in the cell named CHOICE. The macro then checks that cell. If the user typed Y, the macro branches to the macro named SOME_MORE. If the user typed N, the macro branches to NO_MORE. If the user typed some other key, the macro branches to ASK_AGAIN, which could display the message again and wait for either a Y or an N.

{ifkey *s*}   This command is similar to the {if} command, but it returns a true result if *s* is a valid macro name for a key, such as UP, PGDN, CALC, or HOME. You will generally use this command when writing a macro that refers to a named cell that contains a macro key name, which the macro can check and act on accordingly. For example, the first line of

```
{get CHOICE}
{ifkey @mid(CHOICE,1,@length(CHOICE)-2)}{branch MORE}
```

pauses until the user presses a key, and then stores that key in the cell named CHOICE (the Home key is stored as {HOME}, the ↑ key as {UP}, and so on). The {ifkey} command then checks that cell with the @mid function, which ignores the beginning and ending curly braces. If the cell contains a macro keyname, such as HOME or UP, it then branches to the routine named MORE.

{look *loc*}   This command checks for keyboard activity during macro execution by looking for keystrokes in the computer's keyboard buffer. If a key was pressed, the character or the macro-equivalent, such as {HOME}, is entered in *loc*. The macro takes no action on the keystroke, and the keyboard buffer is not cleared, so the spreadsheet will eventually receive that keystroke. For example, the routine

```
{blank CHOICE}
{PRINT_ONE}
{look CHOICE}
{if @length(CHOICE)>0}{get CHOICE}{ASK_STOP}
{PRINT_TWO}
```

first erases the cell named CHOICE, and runs the first print routine, PRINT_ONE. If the user has pressed any key during the print routine, the {look} command copies that keystroke to CHOICE. The next line checks CHOICE, and if it contains anything, the {get} command eliminates the keystroke from the computer's keyboard buffer, and then runs the macro ASK_STOP. This macro could then ask the user if it should stop printing. If no key was pressed, or ASK_STOP is told to continue, the routine named PRINT_TWO is run.

{menubranch *loc*}   This command gives control to the macro menu at *loc*. That macro menu must be structured as a menu or problems will result. For example, the routine

```
{if @month(@now)=1}{menubranch JAN_MENU}
```

branches to the menu named JAN_MENU if the current month is January.

{menucall *loc*}   This command is similar to {menubranch}, except that the menu is called as a subroutine. When any macro associated with the menu is finished, control will return to the first command after {menucall}. For example, the routine

{menucall JAN_MENU}
{DO_CONTINUE}

calls the menu named JAN_MENU, and when the macro at that menu is finished, control returns to the next line, which calls a macro named DO_CONTINUE.

{message *loc,col,row,time*} This command displays the contents of *loc* as a message in a box, whose upper-left corner begins at screen position *col* and *row*. The message is displayed until *time*. Entering a *time* of 0 seconds displays the message until the user presses a key. The width of the message box is determined by the width of *loc*'s column. For example, the macro

{message MESSAGE1,30,10,@NOW+@TIME(0,0,5)}

displays the contents of the block named MESSAGE1 in a box that begins at column 30 and row 10, near the center of the screen. The message is displayed for 5 seconds.

{play "*filename*"} This command plays the digitized sound file "*filename*." Note that *filename* must appear in quotes.

{stepoff}–{stepon} This command toggles the macro debugger's single-step mode. This has the same effect as the Tools-Macro-Debugger-No or Yes command. You can run a macro at normal speed, and it will go into single-step mode when it reaches the {stepon} command. It will proceed step by step until the macro finishes or a {stepoff} is encountered.

{wait *time*} Pauses the macro until *time*. No keystrokes will be processed during the pause. Enter *time* as a value for a specific point in time, not as a number of minutes or seconds. For example,

{wait @NOW+@TIME(0,0,10)}

pauses for 10 seconds.

PROGRAM CONTROL

These macro commands control the flow of the program, and contain the basic elements of any programming language. They provide the tools that turn your keyboard macros into full-fledged programs.

{; *item*} When a semicolon is the first character within the braces, any other characters in *item* will be interpreted as a comment, and the macro will ignore this line of code. Use comments for documentation, reminders, or place holders for future macro editing. You can also use two empty braces, {}, as place holders.

{branch *loc*} This command passes control to the macro at *loc*. For example, in the routine

{if QTR_TOTAL>GOAL}{branch GRAPH_QTR}
{GRAPH_GOAL}

if the contents of the cell named QTR_TOTAL is greater than that in GOAL, the macro branches to the routine named GRAPH_QTR. Because it is a {branch} command, the macro will not return to this point. Therefore, the only circumstance in which {GRAPH_GOAL} will be run is if QTR_TOTAL is less than GOAL and the {branch} macro is not run.

{define *loc1:t,loc2:t*...} This command denotes the locations for storing arguments passed when another macro calls it as a subroutine. The type *t* can be Value or String. When a macro calls a subroutine, it can pass that routine information in the form of arguments. For example, the macro command line

{MACRO4 44,"some text",SOME_CELL}

calls a macro named MACRO4, and passes it three parameters: a value, a string, and a block name. In order to accept these parameters, the first line of MACRO4 should contain a {define} statement, such as

{define VAR1:value,VAR2,VAR3:value}

This statement places the first argument, 44, as a value in the cell named VAR1. The string *some text* is placed in the cell VAR2. Because VAR3 is given a type of Value, the contents of SOME_CELL is placed in VAR3 (assuming SOME_CELL contains a value).

{dispatch *loc*} This command branches to the macro whose address or block name is entered into the cell at *loc*. It is similar to the @@ function in that it makes an indirect reference to the macro via the intermediate cell. For example, in the routine

> {getlabel "Enter you initials, such as CPW- ",CHOICE}
> {dispatch CHOICE}

the first line prompts the user for input, and stores it in the cell named CHOICE. The {dispatch} command then looks at the contents of CHOICE, and branches to the macro of that name. If the user entered the initials ACP, the {dispatch} macro would branch to a macro named ACP.

{for *counter,start,stop,step,loc*} This command repeats a macro a specified number of times. It invokes the subroutine at the cell *loc* and repeats it for each *step* between *start* and *stop*. The current count is stored in the cell *counter*. For example, the routine

> {for VAR,1,10,1,LOOP}

executes the macro named LOOP 10 times (the count runs from 1 to 10 and steps 1 for each loop). The number of each loop, starting with 1, is stored in the cell named VAR.

{forbreak} This command cancels the looping of the {for} macro and returns control to the next command after the {for} statement.

{if *cond*} This command is similar to the @IF function. The *cond* is a logical expression that the macro evaluates. If the expression is false, execution continues with the next cell below, skipping any other commands in the same cell as the {if} command. If the expression is true, the macro executes any other commands in that cell. If the true statement does not branch to another macro, the macro in the cell below will be executed next. For example, in the routine

> {if VAR>10}{branch CONTINUE}
> {DO_MORE}

if the contents of the cell named VAR are greater than 10, the macro will branch to CONTINUE. Otherwise, the macro will proceed to DO_MORE.

{onerror *macro-loc,(message-loc)*} This command traps a system error (which would normally halt macro execution) and branches to the macro in *macro-loc*. You can place the error message that Quattro Pro generates into *message-loc*. For example, in the routine

    {onerror CATCH_ERR,SHOW_ERR}
    {GET_FILE}

if an error occurs during the GET_FILE routine, macro execution will branch to CATCH_ERR. The error message that Quattro Pro generates, such as *File not found* will be placed in SHOW_ERR.

{quit} This command stops the macro execution and returns to Ready mode. A blank cell or a numeric entry will also stop macro execution, but the {quit} command ensures that you will know exactly where the macro should stop.

{restart} This command clears all subroutine layers (subroutines can call other subroutines to as many as 32 layers deep) and resets the hierarchy to its default status. Use {restart} to break out of a subroutine or {for} statement and cancel the tie to the calling macro. Execution continues immediately with the command following the {restart} statement.

{return} In a subroutine, this command returns control to the calling macro. Although it is not required (control is returned when the subroutine is finished), including {return} provides a visual end to the macro subroutine.

CELL MANIPULATION

These macro commands manipulate spreadsheet cells. For example, you can use the {blank} command to erase cells and the {recalc} command to recalculate cells.

{blank *loc*} This command erases the block *loc*. The {blank} command can be accessed from any mode (unlike the Edit-Erase command), such as while editing a cell or selecting items from the Quattro Pro menus. For example,

   {blank QTR_4}

erases the contents of the block named QTR_4.

{contents *target,source,(w),(f)*} This command places the contents of the *source* cell in the *target* cell, but always as a string. You can optionally specify a width, *w*, and a format style, *f*, to make the resulting string look like the source number with a numeric format. For example,

   {contents OTHERCELL,FIRSTCELL,9,120}

places the contents of FIRSTCELL in OTHERCELL as text, using a cell width of 9 and a format number of 120. Format style 120 is a Time format. If FIRSTCELL contained the @NOW function, running the macro at 8:30 in the morning would place the text *08:30 AM* in OTHERCELL. See the Quattro Pro @ *Functions and Macros* reference manual for the numbers of the numeric format styles.

{let *loc,item(:t)*} This command places *item* in *loc*. You can optionally specify the type *t* as either String or Value. If *item* is a cell address or name, the {let} command places the contents of that cell in the cell at *loc*. If the source cell contains a formula, only the result of the formula is placed into *loc*. Also, unlike the spreadsheet's Edit-Copy or Edit–Value command, it does not copy all cell attributes to the destination.

{put *loc,col,row,item:t*} This command places *item* in the cell at the *col* and *row* offset in the block named *loc*, as optional type *t*. For example,

   {put A1..D10,2,3,16+5}

places the value 21 (the result of the formula) in cell C4. The column and row numbers are counted as offsets from the first cell of the block named in loc. Column C has an offset of 2 from the first column in the block (A), and row 4 has an offset of 3 from the first row in the block (1).

{recalc *loc,(cond),(n)*} This command recalculates the cells in *loc* row by row, thereby avoiding the need to recalculate the entire spreadsheet. If the two optional arguments are not included, just one recalculation will occur. With the options, it repeats the recalculation up to *n* times or as long as *cond* is true.

{recalccol *loc,(cond),(n)*}   This command is the same as the {recalc} command, except that recalculation occurs column by column instead of row by row.

TEXT FILES

These commands are quite similar to the file commands found in BASIC and other programming languages. You can manipulate only one text file at a time, and you specify that file with the {open} command. Once a file is open, all other file commands will act only on that file. To work on a second file, you must use the {close} command to close the file that is currently open, and then open the other one.

{close}   This command closes the currently opened text file. This command takes no parameters, since only one file can be open at a time.

{filesize *loc*}   This command enters the file size (in bytes) in the cell at *loc*.

{getpos *loc*}   This command enters the current file pointer position (in bytes) in the cell at *loc*.

{open *filename,access-mode*}   This command opens the text file *filename* for future manipulation by the other file macro commands. The *access-mode* can be Write, Read, or Modify, as well as Append (not available in Lotus 1-2-3). These can be abbreviated to W, R, M, or A. If the command fails (because you misspelled the file name, for example), macro execution continues in the same cell. Otherwise, execution continues in the next cell below. For example:

```
{open "MYFILE.TXT",R}{branch NO_FILE}
{readln RECORD1}
```

opens the file named MYFILE.TXT in the current directory, as a read-only file. If the file does not exist, the macro will branch to NO_FILE, which could prompt the user about the problem. If the file does exist, the macro ignores the {branch} and continues with the {readln} command.

{read n,loc} This command reads *n* number of bytes (characters) from the currently open file and places the text in the cell at *loc*. The bytes that are read are those that begin at the current pointer location in the file (as indicated by the {getpos} command).

{readln loc} This command is the same as {read}, except that you do not specify a number of bytes. Instead, all the bytes from the file pointer's position to the end of the current line are read and placed in the cell at *loc*.

{setpos n} This command positions the file pointer on byte number *n*, where byte 0 is the first byte in the file. For example, the routine

```
{open "TEXTFILE.PRN",R}
{setpos COUNTER}
{read WORD_SIZE,SOME_TEXT}
```

opens the file TEXTFILE.PRN for read-only, and sets the file pointer at the byte number shown in the cell named COUNTER. The third line reads the number of bytes shown in the cell named WORD_SIZE and places the text into the cell named SOME_TEXT.

{write s1,s2...} This command writes the string *s1*, which should be enclosed in quotes, into the currently opened file at the file pointer's position in that file. To write more than one string, separate each string from the next with a comma, up to a maximum of 254 characters. For example, the routine

```
{open "TEXTFILE.PRN",M}
{setpos COUNTER}
{write SOME_TEXT,MORE_TEXT}
```

opens the file TEXTFILE.PRN for modification, and sets the file pointer at the byte number that is shown in the cell named

COUNTER. The third line writes the text from cell SOME_TEXT into the file at the current pointer position, and then follows that with the text from cell MORE_TEXT.

{**writeln** *s1,s2*...} This command is the same as {write}, except that the characters for a carriage return and line feed are entered after the text.

INDEX

@@ function, 207
; (semicolon) macro command, 235
/ (slash) key, 9

A

@ABS function, 199
absolute cell addresses, 195–196
@ACOS function, 199
alignment, label, 89
area graphs, 69
arrow keys, 6–7, 10
ASCII file importing, 142
ASCII file output, 107
@ASIN function, 199
aspect ratio
    graph, 112
    screen, 95
@ATAN function, 199
@ATAN2 function, 199
autoload file, 102
Autoscale fonts, 93
@AVG function, 202

B

banner orientation, 116–117
bar graphs, 69
    bar width in, 63–64
    combining with line graphs, 65
    rotated, 70
    stacked, 70
beep control, 102
beep macro command, 230
binary file output, 108, 111
blank macro command, 238
blocks, 13
    applying fonts to, 125
    character searching in, 20–21
    complex criterion
        searching in, 21
    copying, 30–31, 43–44, 140
    defining, 19–20
    deleting records from, 22
    erasing contents of, 32–33
    extracting records from, 22–23,
        25–26, 155–156
    filling, 33–34
    keyboard definition of, 14
    keyboard highlighting of, 14–15
    locating records in, 23–24
    mouse highlighting of, 14–15
    moving, 35–36
    naming, 36–39
    naming columns in, 18–19
    printing, 105–106, 119–120
    reformatting, 150
    saving to a file, 155–156
    shading in, 134
    sorting rows in, 27–29
    spreadsheet linking and, 15–16,
        139–140
    transposing, 42
branch macro command, 235
breakoff/breakon macro
    command, 231
bullet characters, 82

C

@CELL function, 207
@CELLINDEX function, 208
@CELLPOINTER function, 208
cells, 5–6
    absolute addresses of, 195–196
    attribute determination of, 207–208
    circular references in, 101
    copying, 30–31, 43–44

data entry in, 16–17
erasing contents of, 32–33
grid pattern around, 128–129
macro manipulation of, 237–239
numeric format of, 89, 129–132
printing contents of, 110
protected, 26–27, 33, 100, 132–133
referencing, 82, 195–197, 228–229
relative addresses of, 196
requesting information about, 207–208
shading of, 134
text alignment in, 120–121
@CHAR function, 209
@CHOOSE function, 205
circular references, 101
@CLEAN function, 209
clock display, 98
close macro command, 239
closing, 44–46
@CODE function, 209
colors, screen, 86–87
@COLS function, 208
column graphs, 69
columns
  borders display for, 160
  deleting, 31–32
  hiding, 126–127
  inserting, 34–35
  locking, 159
  naming, 18–19
  parsing labels into, 148–150
  reformatting, 150
  transposing, 42
  width of, 89, 121–122, 124, 133–134
comma-delimited files, 142
compression, file, 60–62
contents macro command, 238
copying
  blocks, 30–31, 43–44, 140
  cells, 30–31, 43–44
  files, 186, 188
  formulas as values, 43–44
  graphs, 75
@COS function, 200
@COUNT function, 202–203
@CTERM function, 217
Ctrl-Break key, 10
Ctrl-key combinations, 10
currency format, 95–96
cursor
  keyboard control of, 6–7
  mouse control of, 8–9
@CURVALUE function, 225

D

data entry, 16–17
@DATE function, 213
date functions, 212–216
date/time format, 96
@DATEVALUE function, 213–214
@DAVG function, 224
@DAY function, 214
@DCOUNT function, 224
@DDB function, 217
define macro command, 235–236
@DEGREES function, 200
deleting. *See also* erasing
  columns, 31–32
  files, 187–188
  rows, 31–32
directory
  default, 46, 102, 192
  tree, 193–194
dispatch macro command, 236
@DMAX function, 224
@DMIN function, 224
DOS Shell command, 58–60
draft graphics quality, 90
drawing pad, 164–165
drawing toolbox, 165
drop shadow, 78, 83
@DSTD function, 224
@DSTDS function, 224

@DSUM function, 224
@DVAR function, 224
@DVARS function, 224

E

editing keys, 8
End key, 7
erasing. *See also* deleting
    block contents, 32–33
    cell contents, 32–33
    spreadsheet, 47
    undoing, 33, 43
@ERR function, 221
Escape key, 10
@EXACT function, 209
exiting, 48
expanded (EMS) memory, 4, 91, 98–99, 225
@EXP function, 200
extensions, file name, 55–56, 103

F

@FALSE function, 221
Fast Graph command, 67–68
@FILEEXISTS function, 221
files
    compression of, 60–68
    copying, 186, 188
    deleting, 187–188
    displaying list of, 191–192
    displaying tree structure of, 193–194
    File Manager window, 183–186
    importing, 141–142
    opening, 49–52, 190
    printing list of, 192
    renaming, 187, 189
    sorting list of, 193
    subdirectory creation, 190–191
filesize macro command, 239
filling, 33–34
final graphics quality, 90

financial functions, 216–221
@FIND function, 210
fonts, 125–126
    Autoscale, 93
    on graphs, 82–83, 179
    LaserJet, 93
    quality of, 89–90
    zoom size of, 104
footers, 115
forbreak macro command, 236
for macro command, 236
format defaults, 88–89
frequency distribution table, 140–141
function keys, 10
functions, 198. *See also names of individual functions*
    date, 212–216
    financial, 216–221
    mathematical, 199–202
    session query, 225
    statistical, 202–204, 223–224
    string, 208–212
    table-lookup, 204–206
    time, 212–216
@FV function, 217
@FVAL function, 217

G

gallery, 166
getlabel macro command, 231
get macro command, 231
getnumber macro command, 232
getpos macro command, 239
graph button, 174, 179–180
graphchar macro command, 232
graphics quality, 89–90
graphs
    annotation of, 163–166
    area, 69
    autosave and, 73
    background color, 77–78
    background of, 173–174

bar. *See* bar graphs
circle drawing on, 169
clip art on, 167–168
colors in, 64–65
column, 69
copying, 75
copying objects between, 167–168
data-point styles on, 64–65
data series definition, 79–80
drawing arrows on, 166
ellipse drawing on, 168–169
fast display of, 67–68
file types for, 113
fill patterns for, 64, 66
fonts on, 82–83, 179
grid for, 78
high-low, 69
inserting, 71–72
interior labels on, 64, 66
line, 70
line drawing on, 170, 180–181
line styles on, 64–65
linking objects on, 170–171
moving objects on, 171–174
naming, 73–76
outlining, 78
pie, 65–66, 70
polygon drawing on, 175
polyline drawing on, 175–176
printing, 111–113
rectangle drawing on, 177
removing, 71
resetting definition of, 66
scale of, 84–85
secondary y-axis on, 66–67
slide shows and, 76–77
text entry on, 178–180
text on, 80–83
three-dimensional, 70, 79
updating, 66
viewing, 83
x-axis appearance, 84–86
x-axis definition, 79–80
xy, 70
y-axis appearance, 84–86
grid drawing, 128–129
grid lines, removing, 159

H

headers, 115
help function, 10–11
@HEXTONUM function, 210
high-low graphs, 69
@HLOOKUP function, 205–206
@HOUR function, 214

I

@IF function, 222
ifkey macro command, 232–233
if macro command, 236–237
@INDEX function, 206
indicate macro command, 230
input line, 5
inserting
    columns, 34–35
    graphs, 71–72
    rows, 34–35
installation, 2–3
@INT function, 200
@IPAYMT function, 217
@IRATE function, 218
@IRR function, 218
@ISERR function, 222
@ISNA function, 222
@ISNUMBER function, 222
@ISSTRING function, 222

L

landscape orientation, 112, 116
LaserJet fonts, 93
@LEFT function, 210
@LENGTH function, 210
let macro command, 238

LICS (Lotus International
    Character Set), 96
linear regression analysis, 137–138
line drawing, 128–129
    on graphs, 170, 180–181
line graphs, 70
linking formulas, 139–140, 151–152,
    197–198
@LN function, 200
@LOG function, 200
logical operators, 221–223
look macro command, 233
Lotus International Character Set
    (LICS), 96
@LOWER function, 210

M

macros, 143
    breakpoints in, 143–144
    cell manipulation with, 237–239
    cell referencing in, 228–229
    character codes in, 227–228
    command language syntax, 229
    debugging, 143–144
    executing, 145
    interactive control with, 231–234
    Lotus 1-2-3, 145
    menus in, 228, 233–234
    naming, 146
    parameters in, 229
    program flow control with, 235–237
    recording, 146–147
    replaying, 145
    screen control with, 230
    screen rewrite and, 99
    startup, 103
    text file manipulation with, 239–241
map view, 160
math coprocessor, 91
mathematical functions, 199–202
mathematical operators, 195–196

matrices
    inverting, 135
    multiplying, 135
@MAX function, 203
@MEMAVAIL function, 225
@MEMEMSAVAIL function, 225
memory requirements, 91
memory-resident programs, 59
menubranch macro command, 233
menucall macro command, 233–234
menu selection, 9–10
menu tree options, 103
message macro command, 234
@MID function, 210
@MIN function, 203
@MINUTE function, 214
@MOD function, 201
@MONTH function, 214
mouse button, 91–92
mouse functions, 7–9
    block highlighting, 14–15
mouse palette, 8–9, 97–98

N

@NA function, 223
names, block, 36–39
names, graph, 73–76
negative number format, 96
@N function, 210
@NOW function, 215
@NPER function, 218
@NPV function, 218
numeric format, 89, 129–132
@NUMTOHEX function, 210

O

onerror macro command, 237
opening files, 49–52, 190
open macro command, 239–240
operators
    logical, 221–223
    mathematical, 195–196

optimization, 136
orientation, 112
output block, 24–25

P

page layout, 114
    footers, 115
    headers, 115
    margins, 115–116
    orientation, 116
    page breaks, 114, 127–128
    page fit, 115, 118–119
    scaling, 117
paneloff/panelon macro command, 230
Paradox Access, 17–18, 99–100
parsing, 148–150
path, default, 46
@PAYMT function, 219
pie graphs, 65–66, 70
@PI function, 201
play macro command, 234
plotters, 94
@PMT function, 219
portrait orientation, 112, 116
@PPAYMT function, 219
printer installation, 92–94
printing
    blocks, 105–106, 119–120
    cell contents, 110
    column headings for, 113–114
    graphics quality, 108
    graphs, 111–113
    multiple copies, 106
    output destination, 107–109
    page breaks, 127–128
    page layout. *See* page layout
    row headings for, 113–114
    screen preview, 108–109, 111
    setup string for, 117–118
program flow control, 235–237
@PROPER function, 211
property sheet, 165–166

protected cells, 26–27, 33, 100, 132–133
protected spreadsheets
    opening, 51–52
    saving, 54
punctuation format, 96
put macro command, 238
@PV function, 219
@PVAL function, 219–220

Q

quick keys, 10
quit macro command, 237
quote-delimited files, 142

R

@RADIANS function, 201
@RAND function, 201
@RATE function, 220
readln macro command, 240
read macro command, 240
recalc macro command, 238–239
recalccol macro command, 239
recalculation, 100–102
regression analysis, 137–138
relative cell addresses, 196
@REPEAT function, 211
@REPLACE function, 211
replacing characters, 39–42
Reset command, 25
restart macro command, 237
retrieving, 52–53
return macro command, 237
@RIGHT function, 211
@ROUND function, 201
rounding, 130–132
rows
    borders display for, 160
    deleting, 31–32
    height of, 122–123
    inserting, 34–35
    locking, 159

transposing, 42
@ROWS function, 208

S

saving, 53–58
    blocks, 155–156
    a protected spreadsheet, 54
screen colors, 86–87
screen modes, 87–88, 94–95
screen preview, 108–109, 111
scroll bar, 9
scroll box, 9
searching
    case sensitive, 41
    character, 20–21
    complex criterion, 21
    replacing characters and, 39–42
@SECOND function, 215
semicolon (;) macro command, 235
setpos macro command, 240
@S function, 211
shading, 134
Shell command, 58–60
shortcut keys, 10
@SIN function, 201
slash key (/), 9
slide shows, 76–77
@SLN function, 220
snow, 95
sorting
    files list, 193
    order of, 29–30, 96–97
    rows, 27–29
@SQRT function, 201
SQZ! command, 60–62
statistical functions, 202–204, 223–224
status box, 166
status line, 6
@STD function, 203
@STDS function, 203
stepoff/stepon macro command, 234
@STRING function, 211–212
string functions, 208–212
string searching, 39–42
subdirectories, making, 190–191
@SUM function, 204
@SUMPRODUCT function, 204
@SYD function, 220

T

table-lookup functions, 204–206
table of calculations, 152–155
@TAN function, 202
@TERM function, 220–221
terminate-and-stay-resident programs, 59
three-dimensional graphs, 70, 79
time/date format, 96
@TIME function, 215
time functions, 212–216
@TIMEVALUE function, 215
@TODAY function, 215
transposing, 42
tree structure display, 193–194
@TRIM function, 212
@TRUE function, 223

U

Undo command, 33, 43
@UPPER function, 212

V

@VALUE function, 212
@VAR function, 204
variable reevaluation, 150–151
@VARS function, 204
@VERSION function, 225
video modes, 87–88, 94–95
@VLOOKUP function, 206

W

wait macro command, 234
what-if table of calculations, 152–155

wildcard characters, 184–185, 221
windows
    changing active, 161
    File Manager, 183–186
    juxtaposition of, 162
    keyboard control of, 156–157
    mouse control of, 157–158
    splitting, 158–159
    stacking, 161–162
    zoom control of, 162
windowsoff/windowson macro command, 230
workspace definition, 62–63
writeln macro command, 241
write macro command, 240–241

X

xy graphs, 70

Y

@YEAR function, 216

Z

zoom box, 109

Quattro Pro Quick Keys and Their Macro Equivalents

F: File Manager window only
G: Graph Annotator window only
*: Not available in Lotus 1-2-3

Cursor-Control Keys	**Macro Equivalent**
←	{left} or {l}
→	{right} or {r}
↑	{up} or {u}
↓	{down} or {d}
Ctrl-← or Shift-Tab	{bigleft} or {backtab}
Ctrl-→ or Tab	{bigright} or {tab}
End	{end}
Home	{home}
PgDn	{pgdn}
PgUp	{pgup}

Program-Control Keys	
/	{menu} or /
Alt-*n*	{window*n*}
Backspace	{bs} or {backspace}
* Caps Lock off–on	{capoff}–{capon}
* Ctrl-\ (backslash)	{deleol}
* Ctrl-Backspace	{clear}
Ctrl-Break	{break}
* Ctrl-D	{date}
Del	{del} or {delete}
Enter	~ (tilde) or {cr}
Esc	{esc} or {escape}
Ins	{ins} or {insert}
* Ins off–on	{insoff}–{inson}
* Num Lock off–on	{numoff}–{numon}
* Scroll Lock off–on	{scrolloff}–{scrollon}